Mediation

Mediation

A Psychological Insight into Conflict Resolution

FREDDIE STRASSER   PAUL RANDOLPH
Psychotherapist   Barrister
                         Accredited Mediator (CEDR)

continuum
LONDON • NEW YORK

Continuum   **International Publishing Group**
The Tower Building   80 Maiden Lane
11 York Road   Suite 704
London SE1 7NX   New York NY 10038

First published 2004
Reprinted 2005, 2008, 2012

British Library Cataloguing-in-Publication Data
A catalogue record for this book is available from the British Library.

ISBN 978-0-8264-7503-9

Typeset by BookEns Ltd, Royston, Herts.
Printed and bound in Great Britain

Contents

CONTENTS

CONTENTS

List of Figures

Notes on Authors

Freddie Strasser, PhD, MA, AdvDipExPsych, UKCPReg, BACP registered supervisor, is an Honorary Fellow of the School of Psychotherapy and Counselling at Regent's College, and Director of the School's Adjunct and ADR programmes. He is the co-designer and creator, with Paul Randolph, of the unique Mediation Training Course at the School of Psychotherapy and Counselling at Regent's College, London, which incorporates 'psychotherapeutic' skills into Mediation, and is Joint Leader and lecturer on the course. He is also a supervisor and psychotherapist in private practice. He was one of the first to establish 'existential time-limited therapy', as well as one of the first to bring essential aspects of psychotherapy into mediation. He has written numerous journal articles, and is the co-author, with his daughter Alison, of *Existential Time-limited Therapy* (1997), and the author of *Emotions* (1999).

Paul Randolph is a practising Barrister, called to the Bar in 1971, and an Accredited Mediator (CEDR) since 1999. With over thirty years' experience in a variety of commercial and non-commercial disputes, he now specializes in Professional Negligence and Personal Injury law, although his practice has also included Contract, Employment, Construction, Insolvency, and Property law. His mediation experience covers a wide range of Commercial, Professional Negligence, Personal Injury, Property, Boundary, and Family Financial disputes. Together with Freddie Strasser, he co-designed and created the unique 'psychotherapeutically-informed' Mediation Training Course at the School of Psychotherapy and Counselling at Regent's College, London, where he is now Joint Leader and lecturer. He is a member of the Bar Council ADR Committee, and a trainer mediator on the Bar Council ADR Seminars. He has written several articles on mediation, and has lectured on mediation throughout the UK to barristers, solicitors, local government and other organizations, and to judges and lawyers in Rome, Budapest, and Riga.

Acknowledgements

We would like to express our thanks and gratitude to all those who, whether directly or indirectly, contributed to the writing of this book.

In particular, our thanks must go to Ernesto Spinelli for his mutual collaboration in establishing the principles that sustain the psychotherapeutic aspects of the book; to Emmy van Deurzen for launching us on the path towards the philosophical underpinning of this work; to Alison Strasser who collaborated in establishing the concept of the diagrammatical 'wheels'; to Richard Price and Colin Manning for helping to mould and reshape some perceptions of practical mediation; and to Karen Randolph, Karen Weixel-Dixon, and Oliver Millington for their valuable suggestions, comments, and assistance in editing various sections of the work.

We are also indebted to all members of the Mediation Training faculty at the School as well as the Admin staff who by their hard work and devotion contributed to the considerable success of the Mediation courses, from which much of the material for this book has derived.

Finally, our appreciation goes to Dodi Strasser for the beautiful cover painting which so poignantly reflects the message contained within the book.

F.S.
P.R.

Foreword
The Rt. Hon. Lord Slynn of Hadley

The primary rationale of the authors of this book is to analyse the fundamental purpose of mediation – looking at needs and interests before rights and liabilities – and understanding the very nature of conflict both generally in life and more particularly in the context of the type of dispute with which lawyers and mediators, and many others, are likely to be concerned.

For the larger part it is an essentially practical book with clear advice on how a mediation should be prepared, how the statement of issues should be written, when the mediator should see the disputants together and when separately, whether the lawyer or party or its representative should speak, how the mediator should maintain his or her neutrality and not become too involved - in a word, how to avoid the pitfalls.

But to provide a **vade mecum** is only a part of the authors' purpose, perhaps in their minds the secondary part. After what they term a 'gallop through the ages of philosophical thought' – it is indeed a gallop and given the size of the book it could only be a gallop, and an interesting one – they stress the importance of understanding the psychology of conflict and reconciliation. In other words, the emphasis is on the underlying psychological aspects of conflict and mediation rather than the legal issues. All of this is of greater importance in making the parties and indeed the mediator understand the importance of moving to that 'working alliance platform', where the 'good enough' settlement has become feasible.

Mediation is not simply an alternative – a rival – to litigation in the courts; it has become an adjunct to litigation, encouraged by judges and increasingly acceptable to those in dispute. If it is a rival to anything, it is to arbitration rather than litigation as a way of avoiding the formalities and the technicalities of litigation. But it is not really a rival; it is different and the differences are important. Yet mediation too, if it is to be successful, has its techniques, if not its 'White Book', and any feeling that mediation is simply a question of some amiable outsider blundering into a dispute is dispelled by the authors of this book. They have encapsulated the experience of devising courses in mediation at Regent's College, and of conducting actual mediations. The result is a valuable exposition and guide to those potentially involved, to the parties, their lawyers, and to those chosen to act as mediators.

The first part of the book needs to be read twice – before the 'working' part with all its practical detail, and again afterwards. Each is essential to the other. With mediation being increasingly used, this book, clear concise and readable, will make an important contribution to the understanding of what mediation is about and how it should operate.

Introduction

This book, like the Mediation Course at the School of Psychotherapy and Counselling at Regent's College, represents a relationship in which psychological and legal concepts are combined with the special skills required for conflict resolution – as well as skills for life and 'Executive Coaching'.

It is the result of a realization that 'existential time-limited therapy' has many features in common with mediation, and that the experiences in brief therapy could prove beneficial in all conflict solving, and particularly in the 'caucus' session of mediation, where the mediator speaks to each party in private and in confidence.

This book therefore explores the ways in which a psychotherapeutic approach to conflict resolution can usefully be implemented in the mediation process. It demonstrates some of the ways in which the theoretical and practical concepts borrowed from the theories and practices of time-limited psychotherapy can successfully be adapted for Alternative Dispute Resolution (ADR). It also shows that in so doing, the mediator or 'conflict solver' can be more effective and better equipped to bring about a facilitated settlement of the dispute.

We show how both the mediator and the therapist work in a time-limited environment in which they both attempt to secure a transition from adversity to cooperation, from an antagonistic platform to a 'working alliance'. It is however acknowledged that elements of psychotherapy, though similar in many respects to the ingredients of mediation, also encompass important differences. The therapist or counsellor seeks to bring about a paradigm shift in the client's attitude towards his or her life *in general*, whereas the mediator endeavours to change the party's attitude, not to life, but to his or her approach to the *specific* dispute in question.

The psychological propositions in this book are founded upon a number of basic but fundamental tenets. However, it should be noted that throughout this book the word 'psychology' is used in its generic form. The first tenet is that conflict is ever-present, cannot be eliminated and is part of a natural and necessary cycle of 'conflict and reconciliation'. Linked to this concept is the second proposition, that the very stance of the mediator towards conflict is of itself significant and of importance to the outcome of the mediation: the mediator who acknowledges that conflict cannot be eliminated but accepts that it needs to be 'worked with', is likely to adopt a more effectual approach to the process.

The third essential precept that runs through the entirety of this book is that the mediator can precipitate a paradigm shift in the parties' approach to the dispute through the identification, recognition, understanding and gentle exploration of the parties' 'world-view'. A party's world-view consists of the sum total of that person's values, beliefs, aspirations and meanings, as created in response to the 'givens' or limitations of the world. The parties' world-view governs the way in which they conduct their inter-personal relationships and, importantly for the mediator, will influence their strategies in extricating themselves from the conflict situation. All those in conflict are influenced by hidden or covert motivations as well as having open and ostensible reasons for being in dispute. Through the exploration of the parties' world-view *as it relates to the dispute*, the mediator can reveal these underlying agendas, work with them and help to move the parties from their entrenched positions.

Fourthly, the knowledge and skills set out in this book are effective not only for mediators in mediation, but can also be used as 'skills for life' in all areas where conflict exists, including 'Executive Coaching'.

Mediation is not easy, and the mediator will require all the assistance he or she can muster in endeavouring to move parties from long-held rigidly embedded positions. A mediator with little or no understanding of human behavioural strategies in conflict, and without a proper grasp of the special skills required to work with conflict, can possibly do more harm than good. It is hoped that those who read this book will indeed acquire the knowledge and the skills to equip them better not only for mediation, but also for life.

The phenomenon of conflict and its resolution is considered in the context of mediation, both in the legal environment and outside it. While the book deals extensively with mediation as part of the litigation process, the core objective is to reveal how the use of psychotherapeutic tools can assist a very broad section of the general public in resolving conflicts in all aspects of life, wherever conflict exists. This work is thus targeted at professionals and non-professionals, business people, psychotherapists, students and 'housewives' alike – in fact at all who are involved or concerned in conflict and conflict resolution on a regular basis.

This book closely follows the School's syllabus and incorporates the experiences gained from the years of producing and conducting the Mediation Courses at the School. Just as the methodology of the Courses consists essentially of three elements: theory and discussion, practical and experiential training and mock mediations, so too this book follows that 'trilogy' of approach.

In brief, Part I is a unique exposition of psychotherapeutic theory as it relates to mediation. It contains a brief history of conflict as viewed over the centuries, and furnishes some explanation for the justification of a psychotherapeutic approach to mediation. Chapter 2 also introduces the important concept of 'world-view', a party's outlook on life or upon a particular aspect of life, and demonstrates the importance for the mediator to understand and recognize the parties' world-view. Chapter 3, 'Communication Skills' analyses the psychotherapeutic skills and techniques that a mediator may use in order more effectively to listen to and communicate with the parties, enabling the parties to feel truly heard. It explains the way in which these skills may be deployed to create the optimum prospects for a successful mediation.

Part II provides a more practical, legal and experiential approach to mediation. It sets out the mechanics of and surrounding the process in the legal environment, identifying and explaining many of the procedural problems encountered by mediators. It also contrasts (in Chapter 5 'Negotiate or Mediate?') the essential characteristics of mediation with those of negotiation, highlighting the important distinctions between the two methods of conflict resolution.

Part III contains a series of Case Studies, for use in the mock mediations, which are comprehensively analysed from both a psychological perspective as well as from the mediator's practical and procedural viewpoint. Each Case Study is preceded by a 'diagrammatical wheel', intended as a tool to help in the learning of some of the psychological aspects underpinning conflicts. Each study has commentaries including 'feedback', guidance, hints and advice relating to many of the dilemmas and pitfalls that mediators invariably encounter. The commentaries describe some of the interventions commonly used by mediators, and provide an insight into the more effective – and the less effective – approaches employed. These Case Studies occur at various stages in the School's Course, and the commentaries describe the dramatic learning curve, and the improvement of techniques and approach that students experience as they progress from the start through to the conclusion of the Course.

It is important to note that, although these Case Studies are taken from classic legal cases, they nevertheless represent ordinary everyday conflicts encountered by a variety of 'average' people in the course of their normal lives. The fact that these disputes became landmark legal cases serves only to underline the fact that the parties were unable to resolve them amicably without resorting to the Courts. In this respect they present ideal examples of conflict created and perpetuated by rigid and unbending attitudes.

Part 1

Principles and Theories of a Psychological Approach to Mediation

1

What Is Conflict?

The human race has repeatedly demonstrated breathtaking incompetence in resolving its conflicts. Conflict is an intrinsic characteristic of the human species in every society, irrespective of geographic, ethnic or religious origin. It is therefore remarkable that despite all the advancement of social, philosophical and psychological sciences, man has been unable to develop a coherent explanation of conflict, and even less so an adequate method of resolution and reconciliation.

Conflict shows itself in all human activity and in every relationship that we create. As a result, people have fought their own internal conflicts: family fought family, tribe fought tribe; ancient Greek city fought city and, with the emergence of nation states, nations became the conflict units and fought each other. This pattern has followed human civilization regardless of its cultural and technological development. Many may believe they have a comprehensive understanding of the term 'conflict', yet the most elementary exploration of the term uncovers a tangled maze. The fundamental question 'what is conflict?' generates yet more questions: what is the origin of conflict? Is mankind destined by fate to live with conflict, or can conflict be eliminated? If so, would the elimination of conflict be beneficial?

The interpretation of the term 'conflict' depends upon two primary factors: the vantage point from which the theorist observes the conflict and the environment in which the conflict occurs. There is a vast array of potential environments for conflict: conflict within individuals – or in Freudian terms 'intrapsychic' conflict – when the conscious mind battles with the unconscious mind; conflict between individuals; conflict between families or within families; conflict between nations, between ethnic, religious and geographical groups. In the seminal work *Gulliver's Travels* published in 1726, Jonathan Swift skilfully parodied the range of political conflict in his contemporary society by describing the war between the 'Little-Endians' and the 'Big-Endians', those who opened their eggs from the little end and the big end respectively.

The potential range of problems presented by elements of conflict increases when the inherent emotions, as well as other psychological aspects, are examined. Value systems, self-esteem, freedom of choice, aspirations and meanings, are all extremely pertinent factors relevant to an understanding of conflict; and all are looked at later in this book.

Authors, theoreticians and lexicographers define conflict in a wide variety of ways. In Webster's *Dictionary*, for example, conflict is defined as: 'Clash, competition, or mutual interference of opposing or incompatible forces or qualities'. 'Antagonism' is another way in which conflict is defined. Chambers Dictionary describes it as: 'Agony, antagonism, battle, brawl, collision, combat'. Longman's Dictionary defines it as: 'Disagreement, argument, quarrel . .'. All the dictionaries attribute a *negative* connotation to conflict. Yet, as explored below, not all authors and theorists see conflict in this light.

The way in which mediators view and contemplate conflict will determine their approach towards mediation. The individual mediator's stance in respect of his or her interpretation of the concept of 'conflict' can influence his or her approach and shape the conduct of the mediation process.

A brief history

It may assist the prospective mediator to have an understanding of the way in which conflict has been viewed over the centuries, and so a brief history follows.

Aristotle (384–322 BC)

When conflict is investigated from a historical perspective, it is in Aristotle's philosophy that the first trace of a scientific methodical exploration of this human phenomenon can be found. Some 2300 years ago, Aristotle expressed one of the most enduring metaphors of conflict: the conflict between 'reason' and 'emotion'. Aristotle evolved his 'master and slave' notion, a theory based upon his assumption that emotion and rationality are always in conflict. Emotions, according to Aristotle, are primitive, unintelligent and bestial human expressions; consequently, these dangerous emotional impulses are the slave and need to be suppressed, whereas rationality, wisdom and reason must be the master, firmly in control.

This notion of 'dangerous emotions' has had an enduring influence on Western civilization. The belief that negative emotions cause conflicts, and that conflicts result in 'battles' and antagonism, was prevalent throughout history (Salamon 1993). From this perspective, conflict is a negative human attribute which needs to be eliminated and replaced by reason.

Heraclitus (d. 460 BC)

Even before Aristotle, in the pre-Socratic era, this Ionian philosopher was distinguished by his contempt of popular ideas. His impressive edifice of the universe was built upon the concept of 'change': change being the law of all existence. Change involves opposition and opposition contains conflict. This was in direct opposition to the Pythagorean theorem which searched for the eternal *un*changing laws of the universe.

Heraclitus's texts are concise, pungent and forcibly expressed, in contrast to the sometimes convoluted and tortuous language of many philosophers. Armstrong described his concepts in *An Introduction to Ancient Philosophy* in this way:

> 'War is the father of all things'. The clash of opposites is the very condition of life. Evil and good, hot and cold, wet and dry and the rest are each other's complements and the endless strife between them is the sum of existence. The only harmony possible is a harmony of conflict and contrast. ... For Heraclitus the two members of every pair are indivisible and equally natural and necessary; one without the other is impossible. (1949: 10)

Successive authors, philosophers and psychologists, however, have challenged this point of view, as will be shown below. Nevertheless, some contemporary scientists and psychologists would agree with this paradigm. For our mediation purposes, some of the aspects of Heraclitus's theory, namely that conflict is a natural condition of the universe and is part of the holistic entity of being, should be of vital importance and interest to the mediator.

The Middle Ages

Throughout the Middle Ages, Christian philosophy was preoccupied with the notion of conflict between virtue and sin and between the demonic and the angelic. In the name of these very strong dogmas and behaviour patterns, religious and ideological wars characterized this period of human existence. Conflicts persisted in the name of religion, ideology and the belief in nationhood. Reconciliation followed, but after each reconciliation new conflict emerged.

The notion that conflict must be eliminated and replaced by a unilateral goodness was prevalent throughout this period – as indeed it remains in our modern society. Conflict itself from this viewpoint can be said to be an evil burden that humanity needs to eradicate. And yet despite all Christian and other religious doctrines of love and peace and their endeavour to eliminate conflict, no century has survived without its significant share of war and conflict.

One of the most outstanding conflicts in human endeavour emanated from primary conscious thoughts about the relationship of mind and body. This created one of the great controversies since earliest times: body and soul. Basically, dualism as introduced by Plato, propounded that there are two classes of substance: physical and intellectual – the body and the soul, two different entities unconnected in any unity. The opposite view emerged only in the nineteenth century and was developed in the twentieth century by philosophers and writers who believed in the holistic characteristic of human nature. The contradiction between these paradigms, the clash between the dualistic and holistic view, can determine how people observe and perceive the concept of reality.

René Descartes (1596–1650)

The French philosopher was the one who contributed most to this dichotomy between body and mind. He became a key figure in European philosophy, exerting considerable influence upon scientific realms of existence. Descartes is particularly associated with his pronouncement '*Cogito ergo sum*' – 'I think, therefore I am'. He came to this conclusion through his relentless search for ultimate rational truth. He believed that by the unrelenting questioning and doubting of his values and beliefs, he would eventually find truth. Speaking of his journey through what is sometimes referred to as 'Cartesian Doubt' towards the ultimate truth, he wrote:

> I suppose therefore that all the things I see are false; I persuade myself that none of those things ever existed that my deceptive memory represents to me; I suppose I have no senses; I believe that body, figure extension, movement and place are only fictions of mind. What then shall be considered true? Perhaps only this, that there is nothing certain in the world (*Discourse on Method and the Meditations*, 1968: 102).

7

Thus for Descartes, human beings consist of two controversial entities: the body, including the brain, which is extended and divisible, and the mind, the consciousness that is indivisible. Man is a physical, mechanical body with an incorporeal mind attached in a mysterious way to the body. This dualistic approach to the fundamental nature of reality, dividing the world into two entities, mind and body, has to this day held generally in the Western world from the time of Descartes.

While this dualistic approach to science and philosophy was crucial to the scientific and technological developments of civilization, it has also been challenged by many modern-day philosophers, scientists and psychologists. Furthermore, it has had a negative effect upon social sciences and people's perception of emotions and the interaction between body and mind.

Needless to say, this controversy hugely affects how truth and reality are perceived. In mediation, it is important for the mediator to realize and explore the type of approach he or she adopts in the mediation process. The mediator who accepts conflict as a universal 'given' and works with conflict in a humanistic manner will adopt a different stance to that of the mediator who seeks to eliminate conflict and does not take a holistic approach to conflict solving.

Georg Wilhelm Friedrich Hegel (1770–1831)

This German philosopher also grappled with the notion of truth and conflict. He expressed a theory about contradiction and conflict in a more poignant manner than many other philosophers or scientists. Hegel developed a dialectic process of argument consisting of triads: thesis, antithesis and synthesis. This triadic structure, for which Hegel remains known and remembered, may never have been described by Hegel in such direct terms, but has been so labelled by the post-Hegelian philosophers. The original Greek translation of dialectic is 'discourse' or 'argument', whereas in Hegelian terms dialectic means a process of argument following the structure of the triad. Initially one starts with the proposition, the thesis; when this proves to be inadequate, it generates the opposite, the antithesis. Synthesis in turn absorbs the rational of both thesis and antithesis and discards the irrational.

In terms of mediation, this translates into one party posing his or her view, which can be seen as the thesis; the other party expounding his or her contrary view, the antithesis, and the mediator seeking to combine these aspects in a manner which is valid for both of them, the synthesis, or resolution.

Most of Hegel's writings consist of lecture notes which are difficult to comprehend. Some of his critics like Fichte and Schelling accused him of having 'excogitated magnificent spider webs of metaphysics, but the height of audacity is serving up pure nonsense, in stringing together senseless and extravagant mazes of words' (from W. Durant, *Outlines of Philosophy*, 1962: 257). Yet Hegel epitomizes the inherent nature of conflict in our use of language, describing 'contradictions and contrasts' as the most universal of all relations. In Durant's words: 'Every condition of thought or of things, every idea and every situation in the world – leads irresistibly to its opposite, and unites with it to form a higher or more complex whole' (ibid., 260).

From a psychotherapeutic perspective of mediation, Hegel's concepts are of great significance to the mediator, as will be seen below. For this work's paradigm assumes that conflict and reconciliation belong to those universal 'givens' which cannot be eliminated, but with which the mediator can only hope to work.

Søren Kierkegaard (1813–55)

This Christian theologian lived in a 'golden age' of intellectual and technological activity in Denmark. His life was characterized by conflict and contradictions; he was a pious Christian who clashed with the Church. One of his most perplexing projects was grappling with the difficulties of being a Christian in Christendom. Equally, he disputed the politics, values and culture of nineteenth-century society which was conditioned by the industrial and technological movement and had substituted material ideals for spiritual values.

Most of his arguments were based on the contradictions of things. He argued about the objective and subjective nature of truth: on the one hand, objectivity leads to abstract thought, to mathematics and historical knowledge of a different kind; 'and yet, the objectivity has thus come into being from the subjective point of view at the most either a hypothesis or an approximation, because all eternal decisiveness is rooted in subjectivity' (*Concluding Unscientific Postscript*, 1968: 173). Kierkegaard similarly disputed the scientific methods of ascertaining reality. He found conflict in the belief that human existence is a static mode of being and juxtaposed it with a notion of perennial movement of 'becoming'.

To illustrate Kierkegaard's explorations into conflict, take this quotation from the author himself:

> The existing subjective thinker is in his existential relation to the truth as negative and positive; he has as much humour as he has essential pathos, and he is constantly in process of becoming, i.e. he is always striving. (ibid.: 74)

Kierkegaard thus foreshadowed the twentieth century's existential philosophy, the humanistic psychotherapies and the counselling and existential psychotherapy movements, all of which encompassed the holistic approach to the nature of 'being'.

Emmy van Deurzen (1982: 152–3) wrote of Kierkegaard:

> His writings are particularly relevant today, when most people seem to have reached the same level of doubt and uncertainty about living that Kierkegaard dared to experience in fullness, one hundred and fifty years ago.

Charles Darwin (1809–82)

Charles Darwin was perhaps the first scientist in modern times to include conflict as a part of the natural theory of evolution. Indeed, according to the history of evolution, conflict manifested itself in every step of the gradual evolution of the human adaptation. Darwin postulated the theory that the emergence of humans and other species was 'blind', resulting from the slow, unplanned, cumulative process of selection. The basis of this theory of natural selection was that species mutated according to the survival of the fittest, and that this emerged through competition and conflict. This was in stark contrast to the religious and hitherto accepted theory that the creation of human and other species was God's grand plan (Darwin 1859). According to this view, conflict was there in the plan and had an evolutionary function. In this way, conflict first moved from a strictly negative attribute to a more neutral or even positive interpretation.

Sigmund Freud (1856–1939)

Freud was the first medical psychiatrist whose entire theory was based on 'intrapsychic' conflicts. His exploration of the human mind originated from a medical and scientific point of view, which claimed that the basic human characteristic is the conflict between the conscious and the unconscious mind. The 'id' is part of the unconscious mind and is the repository of unconscious desires and repressed feelings – these are not concerned with external reality. The conscious mind is aware of dangers and is also driven by the 'superego' – which indicates what should and should not be done. These two realms are in constant conflict. For Freud, conflict was a part of the human mind and, like Darwin, he had a neutral attitude to its existence (Freud 1979).

Alfred Adler (1870–1937)

Adler was one the first Viennese psychoanalysts and the founder of the 'Individual Psychology' theory. He worked with Freud for ten years from 1901 to 1911. The differences between these two men were demonstrated both in their theory and in practice.

Adler's core theory rests on the conflict between 'the inferiority and the superiority drives': it is based upon the premise that inferiority is a human basic attribute and, therefore, conflict stems from the human drive to become superior. Adler postulates:

11

to be a human being means the possession of a feeling of inferiority that is constantly pressing on towards his own conquest. (Adler 1938)

Adler's concept of the 'inferiority complex' has in general been misunderstood, not only by the public, but also by psychologists. People have turned to psychologists and psycho-therapists to eliminate their inferiority complexes – in other words the conflict between feelings of low self-esteem and their desire for permanent high self-esteem. Adler states that 'inferiority feelings are not in themselves abnormal; they are the cause of all improvement in the position of mankind' (Lundin 1989). It can therefore be surmised that conflict may be one of the best tools 'for all improvement in the position of mankind'.

Adler's theory proposes conflict as a shared universal condition. However, the possibility of eliminating it exists. Adler therefore sees the inferiority complex as a conflict between inferiority and the drive for superiority – a conflict needing to be cured (Ansbacher and Ansbacher 1964).

Carl Rogers (1902–87)

Rogers was the originator of the 'non-directive counselling approach' in the early 1940s. He was the pioneer of the principle of interpersonal communication between clients and therapists. This was a total departure in the realms of psychology, hitherto dominated by the Freudian psychodynamic and behavioural approaches in which the therapist was a scientific researcher of the patient's disordered mind. The core of the problem according to Rogers, however, was that there is invariably a conflict between the primary positive nature of human beings and the unnatural conditions that civilization imposes on them. According to this paradigm, the many unnatural 'shoulds' (i.e. what should or should not be done) – for example the demands of the family or culture – cause conflict and therefore need to be worked at.

This is how Rogers exemplifies his theory:

As a therapist, I want to make it possible for my client to move in her way, and at her pace, to the heart of her conflict. (Rogers 1987: 151)

For the purposes of mediation, this book accepts and borrows a considerable measure of Rogers' methods and techniques employed in therapy when dealing with human interactions. These are very relevant to the mediation process, particularly in the private caucus sessions, where the mediator uses many skills borrowed from Rogerian concepts.

In hindsight, the boldness and the courage of Rogers is remarkable: he claimed that by empathy, warmth, genuineness, congruence and an unconditionally positive regard, one can establish a therapeutic relationship which is not only curative, but also enables clients to resolve their own conflicts. This was a major departure from psychoanalytical and behavioural approaches.

If, for Rogers, the core problems in therapy were based on conflict, he was also the first therapist who used his 'Person-Centred' approach in conflict solving. Following the Second World War, he was the originator of so-called 'Encounter Groups'. After introducing person-centred methods between two people, he then used the same approach in groups. He was the first to facilitate conflict solving, or what today could be called 'mediation', in Northern Ireland, Central America and South Africa. In 1986, Rogers facilitated intensive group sessions of equal numbers of black and white participants in South Africa. He wrote:

Never have I experienced such depth of rage, bitterness, and pain (on the part of blacks), or such fear and guilt and prejudice (on the part of whites). (Rogers 1987)

This experience was totally contrary to Rogers' theory which held that man's basic nature is positive and good and only needs the correct environment and human warmth to be actualized. In such cases, conflict will simply disappear. For a good and effective human relationship, a person needs 'non-judgmental acceptance of every feeling, every thought, every change of direction, every meaning that she finds in her experience' (Rogers, 1987).

Rogers was thus probably the first successful and effective worldwide mediator. His theories, notions and skills are vital in modern counselling approaches and many of his methods and concepts are crucially important in our mediation model.

Louis Coser (1913–2003)

During the course of the last century, while psychologists and psychotherapists grappled with the question of *inner* psychic conflicts, social scientists emerged and added their contribution to the seminal debate surrounding the question of '*outer*' conflicts. Indeed, such conflict has long remained an unexplored field for social psychologists and social scientists. In *The Functions of Social Conflict* (1956), Louis Coser pointed this out, stating that conflict had been very much neglected as a field of investigation in sociological studies. However, Coser identifies one of the American sociologists, Georg Simmel, as the first researcher to find that conflict has a function, namely a 'group-bonding' character (Simmel 1955). Simmel proposed that conflicts set boundaries between groups within a social system and thus strengthened the group consciousness and 'separateness', in turn strengthening the group identity. This predates the modern social evolutionary scientists' perspective and is remarkable, bearing in mind that Georg Simmel's functional theory was developed at the beginning of the century.

Coser was clearly influenced by Simmel and researched Simmel's theory by refining the functional aspects of conflict in his book *The Functions of Social Conflict* (1956). Coser set out to redress the social scientists' lack of interest; he felt they failed to explore the functional aspect of conflicts. For him, the starting point of social conflict was the struggle over limited resources, with the aim of neutralizing, injuring or eliminating the rival group (p. 8). However, his main theme is that conflict arises between 'us, the in-group' and 'everybody else, the out-group' (p. 35). This conflict, Coser says, does have a unifying function. It creates strong associations and cohesiveness within the respective groups.

This theory transfigures the common definition of the word conflict; it not only puts forward the theory that conflict is part of the nature and condition of being human, but also conveys a positive interpretation, that bonding and cooperation are a by-product of conflict.

Morton Deutsch

Following Coser's groundbreaking theory, Morton Deutsch, a distinguished American social psychologist, further explored the positive and the negative aspects of conflict. In his all-embracing book, *The Resolution of Conflict* (1973), his central theory is not to eliminate conflict, but to make it productive. He draws a distinction between constructive and destructive conflict. He makes the point that in destructive conflicts, the participants feel they are losers because of the outcome. This contrasts with constructive conflicts which produce satisfaction for all participants, creating a sense of gain as a result of the conflict. As an example, Deutsch argues that:

> In some cases, a quarrel between a husband and wife will clear up unexpressed misunderstandings and lead to greater intimacy; in others, it may produce only bitterness and estrangement'. (Deutsch 1973)

This argument reflects the evolutionary psychologists' view that conflict is part of the natural structure of human beings and has its function in the survival of species.

Malcolm Owen Slavin and Daniel Kriegman

Slavin and Kriegman are traditional psychoanalysts with a psychodynamic theoretical background – 'psychodynamic' in the sense that they accept Sigmund Freud's theory based on 'intrapsychic' conflicts. The basic human characteristic is evident in the conflict between the conscious and unconscious mind and where the unconscious is not concerned with external reality. Yet in 1992, Slavin and Kriegman in their book *The Adaptive Design of the Human Psyche* are among the first psychoanalysts who combined their psychodynamic and psychoanalytical therapeutic experiences with the evolutionary theories regarding human nature. These authors see conflicts inherent in their analytical theories from an evolutionary perspective, namely that conflicts are part of the natural human condition and have an evolutionary function. They submit that even in a therapeutic relationship, conflicts emerge as in any other relationship.

> Conflicts are there, because they are part of nature's condition. ... In the clinical context, there is the paradoxical fact that the relationship between patient and analyst is like that between any two individuals, inevitably fraught with pervasive elements of conflicts. (ibid., pp. 157 and 242)

Mediators should therefore also note that in the process of mediation there may be an equal element of conflict between themselves and the parties, as well as possibly within themselves as mediators.

Jean-Paul Sartre (1905–80)

Jean-Paul Sartre is one of the most well-known French existential philosophers of the last century. *Being and Nothingness* (1958) is his greatest work, in which he describes human existence in relation to its world, in relation to itself and in relation to others. He argues that the foundation of relationships between ourselves and others is based on 'reciprocal' and 'moving' relationships. According to Sartre, this relationship in itself carries built-in conflicts. 'Conflict is the original meaning of 'being-for-others' (1958: 364). 'Being-for-others' means the individual's attempt to respect the other on an equal level, though Sartre argues that this very intention creates an experience of difference between individuals, and that in itself is a conflict. Sartre's meaning of 'being-for-others' envisaged a perpetual conflict between others and ourselves. In other words, on a primordial level, mankind is doomed to create conflicts. Sartre thus teaches that every human interaction is in itself a conflict.

Sartre's views on free will are at the very core of the mediation model. Sartre is known for his assertion that human beings are not predetermined by nature, but always have a choice to respond to the determining tendencies. He postulates that even if we do not choose, that is a choice in itself (1958). This aspect of his philosophy plays an important part in the conflict-resolution paradigm, where the parties always have the freedom, albeit limited, to choose a different attitude towards the conflict or to choose a 'good enough' solution.

Edward de Bono (1933–)

The well-known author and psychologist who developed the 'lateral accepted wisdom' theory, developed his view on conflict in 1995 in his book *Conflicts*. He argued that conflicts are due to 'conflict thinking', which is a limited form of thinking and emanates from the dialectical nature of our language. He describes this as an 'argument/clash' of thinking which is translated into a type of communication. According to de Bono, the thinking system, which is based on polarities such as 'good and bad', is inadequate and obsolete for conflict resolution since it is based on conflict thinking: one cannot solve conflict by conflict thinking. He believed that through the self-organizational nature of perceptions, 'idiom' pattern systems are created, which are difficult to transcend and render people's belief system rigid. When conflict occurs in a 'conflict thinking' environment, there is a desire to change it, which is 'wrong'. If there is a claim that is to be opposed, the claim is argued and attacked. In de Bono's words: 'There is the thesis and you bring forth the antithesis' (1995: 19). As a result, each side becomes more rigid, neither side attempts to develop different ideas and an infinite amount of energy is locked up for an infinite amount of time.

De Bono claims that to resolve conflict one must move from this rigidity by lateral thinking. He argues: 'Because any valuable creative idea must be logical in hindsight, we erroneously believe that such an idea would be reached in foresight through better logic. This is nonsense' (1995: 123).

Thus, instead of seeking to prove someone wrong or to 'show someone up' to be ignorant in order to make an impression on others, de Bono proposes lateral thinking. This is a movement from one 'idiom' to another without judgment. He puts forward the idea that this transition can and must be made by suspending logical thinking and risking the exploration and design of ideas which would not normally fit in with logically inspired language. This is based on a system of logic and 'the principle of contradiction'. The ultimate aim is to bring about a fresh insight and change of view. It can be achieved, he argues, by understanding and perception, and by an awareness of the dangers of language.

The alternative to 'argument thinking' is 'design thinking'. In de Bono's words:

> a constructive exploration of the situation with a view to designing an outcome, is in some respects like making a map showing the possible routes and eventually choosing a route. (ibid., 27)

He contends that transcending the thinking system can best be achieved by a third person – such as a mediator. A third party can induce parties to transcend their rigid belief system and facilitate a concept leap. The parties involved in conflict are bogged down by their traditional argumentative mode of language.

Ernesto Spinelli

Like de Bono, Professor Spinelli argues that human beings create values and behaviour patterns which become rigid and difficult to shake. He refers to this human propensity as 'sedimentation' – similar to the coffee squeezed through the filter which remains sedimented at the bottom of the container. According to Spinelli, value and behaviour sedimentations reveal people's 'self-concept'. Sedimentation affects an individual's values, aspirations and behaviour in interpersonal relationships, although they usually resist any disclosure of these. Spinelli argues:

> All sedimented beliefs serve to define the 'self-construct' and as such in most instances, the challenging of these beliefs is highly likely to be met with serious resistance, because a challenge to any part of the self construct also challenges the whole of it. (1989: 349)

Spinelli's view is that conflict is inescapable; but what is more important is clarification of what conflict reveals about the person's sense of being and of his or her values. Needless to say, this knowledge and exploration of sedimentation and values is again a vital feature in mediation, and particularly important for the mediator in the private caucus sessions. One of the aims in mediation is to create a condition that allows the parties to gain an insight into their rigid belief systems and unbending sedimentations – and to challenge them.

Jonathan Sacks

This brief history of conflict would not be complete without mention of Jonathan Sacks' book *The Dignity of Difference* (2002). This provides a further fresh perspective upon conflict and divergence. The book describes the clash of civilizations, the conflict of religions, the positive and negative aspects of globalization and the good and evil of capitalism. Sacks speaks of the pace of change which creates anxiety, which leads to anger and, when combined with deadly weapons of mass destruction, becomes a deadly reality. He investigates confrontations and conflicts, and concludes that without conciliation we will have 'cultural confrontation which results in events like 11 September' and which will repeat themselves (ibid., 3). He writes about religion as a source of conflict, but says that at the same time it can also be a source of 'conflict resolution'.

Sacks further contends that all conflicts have their polarities and that science, globalization, capitalism and even religion have their positive as well as negative aspects. For example, Sacks quotes Francis Fukujama as putting forward a positive aspect of capitalism: 'the fact that it took people's mind away from war and led them instead to the pursuit of trade'. The negative aspect of this polarity, he states, is that it overlooks the great causes that once called forth patriotism, loyalty and the willingness to sacrifice oneself for the sake of one's country or one's faith (ibid., 196–7).

> The danger is therefore that primordial instinct will resurface in revolt against market capitalism's taming of the human instinct to violence. (ibid., 197)

Thus, Sacks guides his readers through many predicaments and paradoxes which mankind encounters. In order to overcome these paradoxes, he introduces an original concept of 'faith, hope and covenant'. 'Covenant' is, according to Sacks, 'the attempt to create the partnership without dominance or submission' (ibid., 202).

> What makes 'covenant' a concept of our time is that it affirms the dignity of difference ... the great covenantal relationship between God and mankind, between man and woman in marriage, between members of community or citizens of society exists because both parties recognize that 'it is not good for man to be alone'. God cannot redeem the world without human participation. (ibid., 203)

Sacks argues that each of us has the capacity to choose how we relate – whether to our spouses, to our parents or to each other separately. This paradigm conveys to us that:

> pluralism is a form of hope because it is founded in the understanding that precisely because we are different, each of has something unique to contribute to the shared project of which we are part (ibid., 203). .... mankind, however, is not merely a 'maximising animal'. We are also, uniquely, 'the meaning-seeking animal'. (ibid., 194)

Sacks' thoughts on conflict demonstrate that he accepts the inevitability of conflict, but at the same time argues that through hope, faith and covenant conflict could be avoided.

The mediator's stance towards conflict

This 'gallop' through the ages of philosophical thought may serve to demonstrate how the common conception of conflict as a *negative* human characteristic can also be seen as an intrinsic positive component of the human condition, and not necessarily a hostile attribute. Conflict thus has a strategic survival function in social and human existence, and this may be important for the mediator to acknowledge.

There is also a corollary to conflict: 'reconciliation'. This has a *positive* human meaning. If, as has been put forward, conflict has a primary 'bonding' function, then reconciliation also has a primary purpose in cooperation and collaboration. Aureli *et al.* put it in this way:

> The most important generalization to emerge from two decades of work on reconciliation (i.e. post-conflict friendly reunion between opponents) in primates is that individuals that reconcile are likely to have a strong social bond. (2000: 307)

'The beginnings of conflict management skills are present at an early stage in children, and cross-cultural comparison indicates the universality of these skills' (Aureli and de Waal 2000: 5). Thus both conflict and reconciliation belong to the natural human condition which is part of the limitations that are imposed upon all individuals. They are 'givens' or, in other words, shared universal characteristics of people's existence in the world. When conflict arises and subsequently subsides, former adversaries have a choice: to reconcile their differences or to perpetuate them. This process is evidenced by the behaviour of many species of animals and primates, as well as in human interaction.

Reconciliation usually takes the form of friendly signals from former opponents and re-establishes a level of mutual tolerance.

Marina Cords and Filippo Aureli ('Reconciliation and Relationship Qualities', in Aureli and de Waal 2000) observed that these friendly reunions also relieve further anxiety and provide a cooperative and bonding function. Indeed, children who participated in their research showed similar patterns of post-conflict reunion and demonstrated conciliatory behaviour in the process of the termination of conflict.

A central assumption in this book, as Sartre postulated (1958), is that simply being in the world involves a perpetual conflict between oneself and others. Further, if reconciliation and cooperation are part and parcel of human existence, then the same applies in mediation. As stated above, a publicly and widely held view is that conflict is an antagonistic human characteristic which needs to be eradicated. If this attitude is allowed to permeate through the mediation process, it leads to a different atmosphere in the mediation to that where the mediator's attitude is that conflict is an integral part of the natural human condition.

Mediators should therefore accept conflict as an inescapable facet of human existence, with the possible consequence of reconciliation. A mediator's desire to eliminate conflict entirely may be an impediment to the ADR process; for the mediator who believes conflict needs to be eliminated will set about the mediation process in a different way to one who feels that conflict is a given in life, that it cannot be permanently eradicated, but that it needs to be acknowledged and worked with. A mediator without this approach may be driven by an over-zealous desire to eliminate conflict and may become assertive or forceful. This is contrary to the manner in which a mediator's skills need to be orientated. Conflict and conflict resolution with reconciliation are natural phenomena seen throughout human history. It is therefore of great importance for the mediator to clarify the attitude with which he or she approaches conflict in mediation.

2

Why Psychology in Mediation?

Mediation models, whether or not they adopt a psychological approach, or have a psychotherapeutic or counselling input, are based upon the premise that all disputes are affected and influenced by psychological or emotional principles – or what the layman might refer to as 'psychological barriers'. All disputes involve injury to feelings, so few disputes will be without their emotional element. If every conflict were approached from a purely unemotional, rational, practical, pragmatic or commercial standpoint, without external influences or other constraints, very few disputes would continue in existence. To remain in conflict with another defies rational scrutiny; to continue in a commercial dispute resists economic analysis. It can rarely be in the commercial or practical interests of any party to be in or to prolong conflict with the other. So what is it that prevents parties from resolving their disputes reasonably, rationally and amicably? What strategies do they adopt to extricate themselves from conflict situations? Why do these strategies so often generate little more than obstacles and blockages to settlement?

Time-limited therapy as the antecedent to mediation

The object of mediation is to help the parties arrive at a satisfactory solution to their conflict – a settlement that is acceptable to each of them. In the psychotherapeutic paradigm of mediation, the aim in conflict solving is to transcend the antagonistic and emotional stance and move the parties from their initial confrontational position to a more reasonable platform. Here they can enter into some form of working alliance, and through this achieve a resolution which is 'good enough' for each of them.

Time-limited therapy

Time-limited therapy involves working with clients in a time-limited way. It follows the concept that time-limited therapeutic encounters mirror much of the finite nature of human existence. The ever-present awareness of 'the ending' can intensify a client's dedication to the therapeutic process, encouraging clients to raise issues and concerns that, in a less time-pressurized environment, they might tend to withhold. Furthermore, a time-limited therapeutic approach may be particularly effective in assisting clients to re-evaluate unduly high expectations of life (Strasser and Strasser 1997, as discussed in Cooper 2003).

In the same way, the application of a time-limited therapeutic approach to mediation can encourage the parties to confront the time-limited nature of the mediation process and to reduce their expectations of the outcome to feasible and workable levels. If such a re-appraisal can be generalized beyond the mediation process, then the parties may develop more realistic perspectives towards all aspects of their relationship with each other and the surrounding circumstances within which the dispute arose in the first place.

The concept of introducing some aspects of a time-limited therapy approach to mediation is important. Yet it is equally important to acknowledge the boundaries between the two. In psychotherapy, the therapist or counsellor seeks to achieve a life-long change in the client's outlook on life (or their 'world-view': their values and value systems, their beliefs, their aspirations and meanings, as created in response to the givens of the world, and which govern how they conduct their interpersonal relationships:

see further on world-view below). In mediation, the mediator aspires not to create a lifelong change in the parties, but merely a more short-term alteration in their attitude towards the outcome of the conflict. Laurence Boulle and Miryana Nesic state:

> While the primary object of mediation is to make practical and efficient decisions about disputes, the primary object of counselling is to address long-term issues of behaviour, growth, or moral development. (2001: 81)

Nevertheless, both the counsellor and the mediator endeavour to produce a paradigm shift in attitude in the parties before them – the counsellor seeking to generate within his or her client a shift in attitude towards their lives *generally,* whereas the mediator is working towards a shift in the parties' attitude to the *specific* dispute in question. It is only when this shift in attitude is achieved that the parties can become ready to accept solutions which they might previously have rejected. For they will have moved to that 'working alliance' platform, where the 'good enough' settlement has become feasible.

In the latter part of the last century, time-limited therapies were developed and became increasingly popular due to the economic and social pressures pertaining at the time. Time-limited therapy forms the basis of the model of mediation discussed in this book. There are a vast number of different therapies, and this model is derived from a variety of them, borrowing certain common ingredients that cut across all models. The core theory is based on an 'Existential' model of therapy: where 'existence' is fundamentally studied and examined ('Existence precedes Essence' – Sartre 1958). Yet research has shown that each therapy has common features: all psychotherapeutic models confront various inescapable and inexorable situations which emulate those facing the therapist and client. These concerns, which both client and therapist, mediator and party all share universally, may be described as 'existential givens'.

It is an underlying tenet of this psychological approach to

mediation that if the mediator is sensitive to these universally shared givens and is aware of their relevance to the rest of the human condition, an empathic relationship can more readily be established between the parties, as well as between mediator and party. Furthermore, by acknowledging his or her own shared vulnerabilities and ambiguities, the mediator can more easily develop a capacity to create the appropriate environment for mediation – one in which the parties can more effectively be assisted in exploring their own limitations, their own vulnerabilities and ambiguities. The mediator's knowledge relating to these 'givens', as will be seen below, is important in the 'caucus sessions', where the mediator explores with the parties the real reasons that underpin and trigger the conflict, and gently seeks to move them from intransigence to flexibility.

The type of clinical psychotherapeutic work explained in *Existential Time-limited Therapy* (Strasser and Strasser 1997) and Mick Cooper (2003) has provided the basis for introducing aspects of this psychotherapeutic approach into the caucus phase of mediation, so as to produce long-lasting results in a short space of time.

Handling parties' expectations in mediation

When parties resort to mediation, their most common motivation is a strong desire to triumph. Similarly, the mediator will equally wish to 'triumph' by achieving a settlement. But of course, *all* parties cannot triumph simultaneously. Each of the opposing parties aspires to achieve the maximum benefit from mediation and the mediator seeks to conclude an agreement between the parties, thereby avoiding litigation. Allowing due respect to the notions of 'positive' thinking and 'win-win' attitudes, all parties in this configuration cannot win. The parties, therefore, need to reformulate what they expect to achieve from mediation and what they mean by 'winning' or by achieving their objective. The 'must win' stance fails to take into consideration some of the universal limitations that the world imposes on the parties, so that such a stance is neither realistic nor attainable.

The mediator and the parties in dispute are all in a relationship in which they are intertwined, sharing the same limitations in the world. They all face individual decisions as to how to respond to these constraints. The confronting parties both believe they are justified and that they have every right to win. The mediator, on the other hand, also carries a strong agenda: a desire to conduct the mediation to a successful conclusion. All these motivations form part of the building blocks of the expectations of mediation.

One important practical rule in mediation that arises from this is that the mediator should consider the parties at the mediation table as individuals, instead of merely as representatives of companies, institutions or nations. In whatever representative capacity the parties attend the mediation, they nevertheless remain individual people, governed by their own outlook and their own individual 'self-concept' and self-esteem. By recognizing these characteristics in each of them, mediators can soon discover the true underlying motives of the parties and their dispute.

Hidden agendas and motivations

One of the most important elements of the mediation process is the exploration of the *covert* reasons for the dispute, as well as the overt. The parties will have developed rigid values and belief systems as their overall strategy for survival in an uncertain world. These can emerge in the dispute as perhaps just a single particular belief. But this might simply be one aspect of an overall overt strategy for achieving a 'winning position'. Beneath this may lie many other diverse motivations: pride, jealousy, anger, hurt, envy, kudos, arrogance, greed, vanity, the protection of identity, self-esteem and numerous other hidden driving forces. These may be precipitated by corporate policies, internal office politics, rivalry between colleagues, family culture or a host of other influences.

Frequently, the parties may not even recognize that the real conflict is hidden and very different to that which they express it to be. They may not understand or recognize their own true underlying motives: they may believe they are simply seeking proper redress or compensation, whereas in fact they are expressing anger and hurt, and a desire to see the other party punished and humiliated.

Take, for example, the demand for money as compensation. This may be born out of a rigid belief system that 'money is the only thing that will satisfy my requirements'. The party may genuinely believe that their requirement for money is purely to *compensate* – simply to restore monies that have been lost or expended as a result of the fault of the other party to the dispute. Yet this demand for money can have a variety of covert meanings in a conflict situation:

to punish	to punish the other party in a way which they believe will hurt most, namely in the pocket
to humiliate	to force the other party to pay large sums of money – 'dig deep into their pockets' – so that they will be publicly humiliated
to vindicate	to demonstrate to the world at large that a substantial award was made, serving to prove that 'we were right after all'
to profit	to obtain a 'windfall' in order to secure a better personal standard of living or way of life or a profit for a business.

The psychotherapeutically informed mediator will thus firstly enable the parties to discover their hidden true motivations and to explore them. Secondly, this mediator will help the parties recognize that they are mutually trapped in a situation which is reciprocally destructive. Thirdly, and perhaps most importantly, the mediator will facilitate the parties to move to a realization that the conflict could be resolved if their attitude towards it were changed – if the platform were transformed from one of antagonistic resentment and distrust to a more cooperative and trusting working relationship.

'Psychological' strategies

The following are a few classic examples, taken from conventional dispute situations familiar to many lawyers, of some common strategies adopted by parties in litigation situations. Although more recognizable in a litigation context, they serve to illustrate the way in which a party's overt stance and actions are motivated and driven by more covert underlying emotions.

Desire for a 'better than expected' settlement

On how many occasions have settlements floundered when the parties seem to be only a small distance apart? Take the following situation:

> Party A has made an offer to settle at £185,000. Party B declares that nothing less than £200,000 will be acceptable. The parties are only £15,000 apart but remain intractable. Party A refuses to increase the offer and Part B still insists on nothing less than £200,000. Neither side is prepared to 'budge' so no settlement can be reached.

If one were to ask either of the parties what the payment or receipt of an additional £15,000 means to them from a commercial point of view, it is doubtful whether they would have a ready answer available. They would probably be forced to concede that, from a purely *commercial* position, the additional £15,000 'would not make a great deal of difference one way or another'. But from a *psychological* point of view, or a self-esteem perspective, it creates a world of difference. Both parties have a desire to come away from the mediation with 'a result' – a good outcome with which they – and everyone involved – can feel fully satisfied. This is particularly so where the parties who attend the mediation do so in a representative capacity, for they are acutely aware throughout the process that they will need to 'sell' the outcome to the organization or body they represent. They therefore hope and aim for a 'better than expected' result in order to secure the commendation and approval that they seek — whether it is from their board of directors, or their boss or their spouse. For whether they represent corporations, institutions or nations, whether they are aware of it or not, people are influenced by their own underlying motives. Thus Party A believes that if he returns with a settlement of £185,000, he will earn commendation and approval, for £185,000 *sounds* so much less than having to pay £200,000. Similarly, Party B knows that a settlement of £200,000 will equally gain approval, respect and admiration, for £200,000 just *sounds* significantly greater than £185,000.

This desire for approval can be said to be part of our need to maintain a 'high self-esteem', and a mediator who recognizes this in the parties will be in a better position to find common ground or to explore wholly separate avenues for settlement.

'Reactive devaluation'
The desire to 'always come out on top' in dispute situations is another example well recognized by lawyers and those conventionally involved in dispute resolution. Yet the desire to achieve 'superiority' may simply be a strategy used in protection of one's own self-esteem. By securing and maintaining superiority, the other party is necessarily and immediately rendered 'inferior'. The lawyers will no doubt recognize in their clients the strategy of striving for superiority by seeking to manipulate the other side — or at least *believing* that one side is manipulating the other. Conversely, they will readily understand that, for the parties in dispute, feeling manipulated is incompatible with feeling superior. The effect of this principle upon disputes can be illustrated by the following example:

> Party A is in dispute with Party B over the installation of a faulty computer system. Party A has demanded either a repair of the entire system, or alternatively a full refund. They would prefer a

full refund as this would allow them to purchase a newer system and would be a neater solution to the whole problem. However, when at the outset Party B offers a full refund rather than a repair, this option suddenly loses its former attraction: Party A instinctively views it with suspicion: 'Why have they offered a refund rather than offering to repair? Perhaps these computers are better than we thought, perhaps they have a good re-sale value?

This situation arises as a result of a value or belief system on the part of the receiving party that 'what is good for them *must* be bad for us'. This phenomenon, sometimes referred to as 'reactive devaluation' (Stillinger *et al.* 1988, as discussed by Mnookin and Ross 1995) occurs where the 'offeree discounts much of what they hear as a self-serving disclosure'. The receiving party 'evaluates' the offer in the light of where the offer originated – and reacts by instinctively 'devaluing' it simply because it originates from their adversary.

The experience of reactive devaluation can not only affect offers and counter-offers at the outset of the dispute, but similarly governs offers and concessions made during the negotiation process or in mediation: where one party makes concessions during the course of negotiations or in a mediation, there may be an instinctive tendency for the other party to devalue such concessions, simply because they originate from their opponents.

Who moves first?

Another classic example of the role of emotional or psychological blockages in disputes can be seen in the 'Who moves first?' syndrome. The desire to be superior and to exit the conflict in a superior position is a strategic barrier that is so often the cause of many an impasse. Take the following scenario with the case of the computers:

Party A has installed a vast computer system at the premises of Party B. The system turns out to be faulty. Party B demands a repair of the entire system. Party B refuses to repair until Party A makes at least some payment: 'Why should we repair goods for which we have not yet received a penny payment?'. Party A refuses to pay before or until they are repaired: 'Why should we pay anything for goods which do not function?'

Parties thus become entrenched in a stand-off which can be of no commercial benefit to either side: the rational, commercial and economic solution would be simply 'to get on with it', for one or other side to swallow their pride and make the payment or effect the repair. Yet the urge to be superior, or the apprehension of being manipulated, prevents each of them making that obvious economic, rational or commercial decision. Such stances may again be born out of the strategies for survival created by the parties to protect their self – their self-esteem, self-worth or self-concept. They are common in many conflict situations, be they commercial, domestic or international. For example, in international or inter-state conflicts, one side is often seen to demand peace negotiations in order to achieve a cessation of violence, while the other side claims that a cessation or renunciation of violence must precede any peace negotiations or else they are futile.

Loss aversion and risk-taking

This is another typical example essentially experienced by lawyers in litigation situations. But it may be important for the effective mediator to be aware of the influences that affect a party's stance towards settlement, particularly in their willingness or otherwise to accept or to refuse offers. What will make one party accept what is 'on the table', whereas another will invariably hold out for more? A considerable amount of research has been conducted in America into these areas of human reasoning, with some significant results. Tversky and Kahneman (1991) considered the effect upon parties of the 'framing' of offers. Consider the following 'mirror' situations:

Party A is owed £50 by Party B. Party B tells A that he can have £50 immediately, or alternatively he can toss a coin: if it lands 'heads' he will receive £100, but if it is 'tails' he will receive nothing.

and

Party B owes Party A £50. He is told he can pay him £50 immediately, or alternatively he can toss a coin: if it is 'heads' he will have to pay him £100, but if it is 'tails' he will have to pay nothing.

The American research shows that invariably Party A would accept the £50 immediately rather than run the risk of losing everything; whereas Party B would prefer to gamble and risk the prospect of paying double in the hope of having to pay nothing. This experiment serves to demonstrate that parties in conflict situations appear to have an aversion to certain loss, and hence are prepared to gamble to avoid certain loss – 'loss aversion'; whereas they have a 'risk aversion' when it comes to gambling and risking loss in order to make a gain.

The above-mentioned research would suggest that in the context of litigation, the claimant is more likely to accept an offer rather than risk going to trial and lose everything (risk aversion). However, the defendant would tend to choose the option of proceeding to trial, preferring to gamble in order to avoid the certain loss (loss aversion). It may explain why claimants, particularly in Personal Injury claims, are frequently prepared to settle their claims at a level that, from an objective viewpoint, would appear to result in under-compensation, whereas the insurers may appear to take on a more robust or intransigent stance when refusing to increase their pre-trial offers.

The psychotherapeutic approach to mediation

The mediator with a psychotherapeutic background or training can recognize and deal with many of these rigid attitudes that so often create emotional obstacles to rational resolution of disputes. These inflexible positions frequently tend to demonstrate a party's shared fears of the uncertainties of the world and the strategies adopted by the parties to respond to these fears. By being aware of and recognizing these attitudes, the mediator can become greatly more effective in facilitating settlements.

Some would say that these emotional or psychological obstacles are created because 'we are people first and litigants second'. As Robert J. Condlin stated (1992):

> We are people first who get angry, depressed, fearful, hostile, frustrated and offended. We have egos that are easily threatened. We see the world from our own personal vantage point and we frequently confuse perceptions with reality. We routinely fail to interpret what others say in the way that others intend and do not mean what others understand us to say.

From a psychological perspective, this may be an accurate observation. However, the mediator will need first to explore how these people exist as *persons* prior to being litigants. This can disclose how they initially reached their dispute and may govern how they react within the conflict situation. Furthermore, by examining how these persons 'function', the mediator can reveal and determine the strategies they have adopted to extricate themselves from the conflict situation.

'World-view'

How does the mediator discover the way in which a person, as a party to the dispute, functions? When a mediator first encounters a party in the mediation, that party is in essence a total enigma to him. The mediator needs to establish, in the shortest possible time, how this individual perceives the various aspects of the dispute. The mediator must therefore ascertain, at least to a limited extent, the person's 'world-view': their outlook on life, and the values, beliefs and aspirations that govern how they conduct their inter-personal relationships. This will reveal their approach to the dispute, their likely attitude in mediation and the way in which they are likely to conduct themselves in order to escape the consequences of the conflict situation.

Webster's International Dictionary deals with world-view as follows: 'Each individual has his own experiences and out of them forms his world-view'. For the purpose of clarifying the meaning of world-view, we need to formalize these experiences and place them into some structural outline.

In order to survive the uncertainties of existence, people create meanings, values and belief systems – beliefs as to what is good for them and what is bad. They also create aspirations and ambitions in order to protect and maintain their self-worth. These are all characteristics of existence. But there is also an element of choice. The values people choose, the aspirations they select, the spirituality they favour are all dependent upon individual choices. People will make their choices according to their value system, and the choices are therefore limited – but they can choose and modify that system. This is an important factor in mediation. For the parties may not be able to change or eliminate the conflict, but they can change their attitude or approach to it. The party always has the capacity to shift a part of his or her world-view. This element of choice, which separates each individual into a 'singular person', is the crux of the psychotherapeutic paradigm – both in therapy and in mediation. These characteristics, which are sometimes referred to by existentialist authors as 'ontological characteristics' (Cohn 1997), bind all human beings together.

Unchangeable givens
What makes up a person's overall outlook or 'world-view'? People's world-view encompasses the 'universally shared givens'. These offer some insight into how this individual reacts to the conflict or dispute, and can provide vital clues to assist the mediator in his or her exploration of the party's attitudes. Some of these givens are unchangeable and unalterable as, for example, the

fact that life is uncertain and unpredictable. These unchangeable conditions include the following, namely that:

- the world is uncertain and inconsistent
- existence is temporal: people are all finite beings, but their relationships and actions are transient
- we are always connected with others and cannot avoid relationships or escape our 'relatedness'
- we all possess a capacity, albeit limited, to exert an element of free will to choose

Each individual in the mediation process, including the mediator, will be subject to these same conditions.

Changeable givens

In contrast to these unchangeable givens, there are other particular conditions which are created and recreated, invented and reinvented by human beings. These are the changeable shared givens. People inherit their cultural values, but retain the ability to create and re-create some aspects of them.

The following are a few examples of changeable givens:

- we create interpersonal relationships
- we create conflicts
- we create our self-image and self-esteem
- we create values and value systems
- we create patterns and strategies to conform to those values
- we may create rigid patterns or 'sedimentations' of our belief and behaviour system
- we create our aspirations
- we have the capacity to create free choices, within certain limitations
- we create our attitude towards our emotional and physical existence

A shared universal given is the fact that we all respond to these changeable conditions. The above structure illustrates some individual responses which are created in the face of some of the unchangeable givens. Each individual has his or her own particular way of dealing with these phenomena, and thus each human being differs from each other (Cohn 1997). The way that we respond to these unchangeable natural conditions defines our world-view. Our world-view, therefore, is the expression of the sum total of these particular givens in relation to our engagement with people and the rest of the world.

World-view from the mediator's perspective

It is important to reiterate the reason for the mediator's exploration of or attempts to uncover a party's world-view. All parties to conflict will invariably have a hidden agenda. They will have concealed motives – some conscious and others of which they may not even be aware – as well as their openly expressed reasons for their conduct. This 'sub-stratum' of the conflict will determine how each party acts and reacts in the dispute and in the mediation.

As previously stated, the mediator is not seeking to achieve a paradigm shift in parties' outlook on life *in general*, but rather an alteration in attitude towards the dispute facing them. So for the mediator, the analysis of the parties' world-view is not some nebulous exploration of their stance towards life as a whole, but is focused upon the specific conflict situation confronting each of them. It is an examination of how the parties engage with each other *and* with the mediator, within the general environment of the dispute and against the backdrop of the conflict. By uncovering relevant aspects of each party's world-view, the mediator will gain an insight into the true motivations and the covert influences driving the parties in dispute. This will in turn provide access to a wealth of information that can facilitate the search for common ground between the parties.

Thus whenever reference is made to 'world-view' in this work – whether as to the mediator's exploration of it or the parties' disclosure in relation to it – it should be remembered that it refers to the world-view as *relevant to and connected with* the conflict and the parties' engagement within it. It is also important to note that whereas a person will at any one time disclose the entirety of his world-view, whether through verbal communication, or by the articulation of his emotions, or through his body language, or other outward manifestations, the mediator and any observer is capable of picking up only a small part or fraction of that person's world-view.

The mediator may also need to facilitate the party positively to *challenge* their own world-view. For it is through this process that the mediator assists them in recognizing their true motives, as well as enabling an understanding of their own vulnerabilities. This in turn renders them more amenable to adopting a different perspective of the problem, possibly seeing it from the other person's point of view.

It is equally necessary for mediators to be mindful of their own 'world-view'. They will need to realize, to some extent at least, how they themselves exist vis-à-vis the mediation and how they respond to the limitations and the above givens. Mediators need to recognize and process their own motivation, aspirations, values and emotions before they can effectively assist the parties. Through this they can more resourcefully engage with the parties and gently steer them to settlement.

If the mediator can come to the realization that the parties are ordinary people facing each other, sharing virtually all the same givens and characteristics – shared not only with themselves but also with the mediator and the world at large – then miraculously, a fresh and more diverse relationship can be created. This then becomes more than an empathic process; it becomes a procedure of mutual validation – a progression where individuals can truly 'connect'.

From this experience of the mediator and the party 'tuning-in' to each other, another more invigorating encounter can develop, where the mediator explores the varied choices available to the parties, albeit within the limitations of the givens. The parties in the dispute exert their free will to choose a solution that may not be perfect, but is 'good enough'. It is then that the parties can feel revitalized, more dignified and their self-image accepted. The initial relationship between mediator and the parties is thus rapidly transformed.

The mediator who is willing to explore his or her own world-view and own vulnerabilities can be extremely successful in this process. In other words, the stance of the mediator – or the therapist – becomes almost more important then the use of the techniques and the skills. The mediator then changes from merely 'conducting' a mediation, to being an ordinary individual relating to the parties in a pure process of mutual exploration to resolve the problem. If this results in a more trusting and empathic relationship, the parties can more easily reflect on their true motivations and also their possible vulnerabilities. This may induce them to change their initial expectations in the dispute, or of the mediation process.

The very essence of the mediator's task is to encourage and enable parties to shift their position. Without such a shift the parties will leave the mediation process in the same entrenched positions as when they entered. This exercise is not an easy one; and the mediator may need all the assistance he or she can muster. It is here that the knowledge and experience of the psychological and psychotherapeutic elements of conflict come to the fore. Through an understanding of these aspects of human existence and behaviour, the mediator may be able to effect a material change in the parties' perceptions of the dispute and their expectations as to the outcome. If they can be moved to a less adversarial position, a greater number of options become acceptable and settlement can more readily be achieved.

Caucus and psychotherapy

The psychotherapeutic elements discussed above are generally employed in the 'caucus' or private session stage of mediation. The caucus is one of the most important components of mediation: it is the stage where, after having seen the parties together the mediator meets privately and confidentially with each party separately (*see further* Chapter 6).

Webster's Third New International Dictionary (1961) defines caucus as 'akin to elder or counsellor'. The caucus session is where the skills and concepts of 'time-limited brief psychotherapy' are employed to establish a suitably secure environment where agreement can be facilitated. It is during this process that the participants are able to reflect upon their private attitudes to the case: what are their true interests in the entire dispute, and how can they extricate themselves from it.

But neither mediators nor counsellors have the luxury of time within which to achieve their objectives. They both work in a time-limited environment and, in order to be effective, they need to create a strong rapport between themselves and their clients or the parties in a short space of time. In the caucus sessions, they need swiftly to build a bond of trust, so that by creating trust they can overcome some of the distrust that has perhaps already built up in the dispute. Counsellors and mediators are both required to work and to deal with strong emotions. Both employ skills or techniques aimed at encouraging openness in order more readily to access underlying motivations, hidden agendas, fears and concerns and other sensitive issues. The more 'high-context information' they can persuade the client or the party to share with them, the easier it is to facilitate the exploration of solutions and options. This is particularly so where in a litigious or antagonistic environment, the parties maintain the belief that any disclosure of their interests and needs will weaken their case.

By adopting this approach borrowed from the model of existential time-limited psychotherapy, the mind-set of the participants can be moved in exactly the same way as in a brief therapy session, where attitudes are considered, addressed and reappraised.

But the mediator who approaches mediation from a psychological perspective should not stray into the realms of the therapist. While possibly acknowledging a party's intra-personal conflicts, the mediator's interventions are more specifically focused upon the dispute rather than any 'world-view problems' the parties might have. The mediator should not 'dig' for intra-personal conflicts if they are not presented. Rather, the mediator will endeavour to explore them if raised, while moving the parties from a fixation with their rights and obligations to an examination of their needs and interests.

It is worth repeating that the mediator's exploration of a party's world-view, unlike that of the therapist, is not for the purposes of achieving a long-term change in outlook. However, in reality these differences between counsellor and mediator may sometimes become indistinct. The possibility cannot be excluded that even in mediation, long-term changes are precipitated in the parties' lives. Many claim to have acquired, through mediation, the knowledge of a 'life-skill'. The experience and skills of counselling can thus usefully be combined with and incorporated into the practices of the mediator. Armed with knowledge of the psychological underpinning of conflict, as well as the psychotherapeutic approach to intra-personal conflicts and inter-personal problems, the psychotherapeutically trained mediator can acquire an 'edge' over mediators without such knowledge or training.

3

Communication Skills

The need to be heard

A common cause of conflict – or at least the escalation of conflict – is the breakdown of communication. Messages simply fail to penetrate the layers of 'communication barriers' (Craver 2001) that the parties create when attempting to 'get their message across':

> What is spoken may not be heard. What is heard may not be understood. What is understood may not be accepted (ibid., adapted from Scott 1981).

One of the many powerful forces that drive parties to litigation is this desire to be heard. They want not just to be listened to, but also to be *truly* heard, *and* understood, *and* accepted:

> The other side have not listened in the past, and they now refuse to listen – that is why we are in dispute. My solicitor listens but he does not truly understand. And no one yet fully accepts our position. But the Judge will listen, and will understand.

Thus the well-known refrain: 'my client wants his day in court' is based upon the desire to be *truly* heard. It reflects an enchantingly naive perception that

- the Judge will listen to me and will really hear me
- the Judge will understand my position

- the Judge will accept that I am right
- the Judge will administer true justice
- the Judge will publicly humiliate the other party with a firm 'rap over the knuckles'
- the Judge will award me substantial damages and thereby entirely vindicate my stance

Many of those who have been through the litigation process will know that such objectives are rarely achieved. On the other hand, many of those who have experienced the *mediation* process will invariably confirm that it really enabled them to be truly heard.

Another difficulty for parties in dispute is that they can sometimes 'mean what they say but not say what they mean, or alternatively, say what they mean but not mean what they say'. In other words, the overt, or expressed, basis of the dispute is not always the true, underlying source of the problem.

So how does the mediator achieve such a high level of 'hearing and understanding'?

Underlying principles to the skills

The mediator seeks to achieve results by building a relationship of trust with the parties, so as to enable them to speak freely, openly and candidly. The mediator will need to create a strong rapport with the parties, but must do so in a short space of time. Below we set out a number of skills or techniques which are generally acknowledged as facilitating and encouraging openness. They are essentially designed to demonstrate and emphasize to the speaker that he or she is genuinely being heard, understood and accepted by the mediator. This in turn can enable the party to 'open up' and to share more freely information which might otherwise go undisclosed.

However, it must be borne in mind that these skills, if used mechanistically and merely as techniques, will not truly serve their purpose. The function of a skill is to be a learning tool, and not a technique in mediation. Mediation is a process of 'being with ordinary people in an ordinary dialogue and discourse'. As soon as a mediator puts on a superior 'mediation hat', it militates against successful mediation – for then the mediator is 'going through the motions of mediating' instead of being part of the process itself. The mediator must therefore acquire the skills and wholly absorb them within his or her own behavioural approach. He or she will then be in a position to deploy the skills in a natural environment, in an unaffected and relaxed mode and in a sincere and spontaneous manner. The parties will thus be best assisted to explore their understanding of themselves, their dispute and their therapeutic interaction.

In order to give perhaps a shorthand diagrammatical illustration depicting a typical mediation process, we can consider the following:

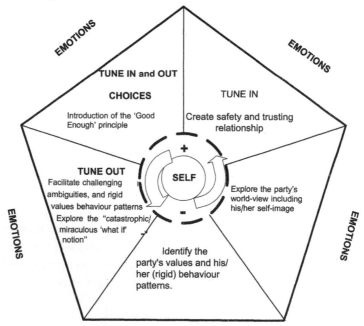

Figure 1 Mediation model in Caucus
(always in relation to the conflict).
The diagram represents a non-chronological and non-linear approach to mediation.

The process described in the above diagram illustrates some of the tools used by the mediator to 'tune in' to the party's perceptual mind and also to 'tune out', in order to see the situation from a greater perspective. The 'tune in' intervention is a form of 'associative involvement' with the other person, allowing the mediator to put himself or herself into the other person's shoes – an empathic relationship involving the validation of the party by understanding his or her viewpoint. It is further supported by the knowledge that the mediator's world-view will, in most respects, be similar to those of the parties. On the other hand, when the mediator 'tunes out' from this associative mode, he or she enters into a more dynamic or active mode of intervention.

One of the purposes of this type of intervention is to facilitate the challenging of ambiguities on the part of the parties. This, however, needs to be a positive rather than a negative process. In the mediation process the mediator will purposefully explore the party's world-view and his or her ambiguity (for example 'I want something, but I cannot have it'). The exploration begins with the 'tuning in' to create a safe and trusting informal relationship with the parties, and it is followed by:

- the exploration of the party's self-image
- the identification of the party's values, behaviour patterns and ambiguities
- tuning out and actively helping the party to challenge his or her contradictions
- prompting the party to consider and explore the 'catastrophic/miraculous "what if" situation': what if he or she were to fail to achieve the expected settlement; or what if settlement could miraculously be achieved.
- assisting the party to move towards and finally accept a 'good enough' solution

The skills

Active listening

There are many ways in which people listen.

'You're not listening to me!'
'Yes I am, I'm just doing something else at the same time.'

For the mediator, it is vital that he or she listens in such a way as to convince the speaker that he or she is 'attending' and giving *full* attention to them. The mediator should never allow the party to believe he or she is bored or uninterested. Student mediators are thus taught a number of non-verbal communication skills designed to demonstrate to the speaker that their message has been truly heard and understood:

Eye contact: a reasonable and appropriate use of eye contact can serve to underline to the party speaking that they are really being listened to. However, the use of eye contact should not be employed mechanically, as for example by a fixed stare; mediators should seek to evolve a manner and style in which eye contact is natural and spontaneous. Mediators should also be aware of cultural differences in approach to eye contact, and care should be taken not to offend or to misinterpret.

Nodding: this can demonstrate an element of *acknowledgment* of what the speaker is saying, thus reassuring them that they have been heard *and* understood. Excessive or inappropriate use of nodding, however, may be taken as an indication that the mediator has more than acknowledged the message, and has even *agreed* with it. This would jeopardize the mediator's impartiality and neutrality.

Posture: appropriate body movement and posture, such as leaning gently forward towards the speaker, can also often help to demonstrate genuine listening and attentiveness.

Interrupting: interrupting the speaker can be a significant barrier to open and fluent communication. Whether it is simply to clarify or to understand, it nevertheless inhibits the flow of information. Interruptions frequently indicate that the mediator has his or her own agenda, wishing to secure some piece of information which may or may not be noteworthy. Alternatively, it can indicate that the mediator has been concentrating on framing the next question.

Silence: silence is a crucial tool in the mediator's armoury and is frequently grossly underestimated. Silence on the part of the mediator provides periods of time for the parties to express themselves freely and provides them with space to contemplate. It enables the mediator to attend and focus upon the party's words, issues and agendas. By *breathing* appropriately, the mediator creates silence, avoids premature interventions and provides space for the parties to reflect upon their own outlooks or 'world-view'. Silence by the mediator can also precipitate a need or desire for the other party to fill it, thereby precipitating the flow of further information.

Open questions

All interventions by the mediator are designed to facilitate the party's free expression, and to enable the mediator to 'tune in' to understand them, to communicate with them and to get into their world. Further, because of the mediator's time constraints, he or she needs to elicit as much 'high-context' information as possible. Thus closed questions, which solicit a 'yes' or 'no' answer, are not 'wrong', but they tend to restrict the flow of information. The information elicited will be narrow, and may serve only to satisfy the curiosity of the mediator. The answer may also possibly be unreliable, for whenever a party is obliged to respond with a 'yes' or 'no', there is the distinct possibility that they will not be truthful, or they will be defensive, or they may say what they believe the mediator wants them to say.

An 'open question' is one that cannot be answered by 'yes' or 'no', and allows the person to disclose a greater breadth of data. From this wide latitude of accumulated facts, the mediator is able to distil and extrapolate the more vital portions of information from the party in dispute.

'Reflecting back'

This involves offering back to the party in a selective way what he or she has said, mirroring or reflecting closely the specific language used by the party. By 'feeding back' to the party what they have said, often using just a key word or phrase, the mediator can show how attentively he or she is listening, as well as clarifying the party's own mode of expression, and checking whether the mediator has properly heard and understood. For example:

> 'I feel that our company was cheated out of income for which we had worked extremely hard.'
> 'Cheated?'
> 'Yes, I feel they have taken advantage of our generosity and easy-going attitude towards business.'

Paraphrasing

The mediator selectively puts into his or her own words what the party has said, but with the minimum of 'contamination' by his or her own subjective values or meanings. The aims of this skill are similar to 'reflect back', in that the mediator shows understanding and acknowledgment:

> 'You seem to be saying that ...' or
> 'What I hear coming from you is that ...'

Reframing

While paraphrasing and 'reflecting back' to the party words they have expressed, the mediator can often utilize the opportunity to 'reframe' the message, by using more neutral words and less confrontational language. This serves subtly to re-orientate perceptions and to shift stances:

> ['. . . and I feel that our company was cheated out of income for which we had worked extremely hard'].
>
> 'So what you are saying is that had the Defendants performed their part of the contract, your company's income would not have been adversely affected . . .'

The above example demonstrates that by avoiding the repetition of the sentiment of 'being cheated' in the paraphrase, the mediator takes the personal animosity out of the message, and 're-orientates' the accusation of dishonesty and bad faith to one of a simple breach of contract.

Summarizing

This involves offering a brief descriptive summary of what the mediator perceives the party to have said. This can be done at any time: after a period of exploration with a party, or at the end of a caucus session, the mediator can pause briefly to 'take stock' of what has been said and restate it briefly to the party. In this way, the mediator draws the various threads together of what has been said. He or she can simplify complex issues and reduce them to a relatively comprehensive list of the important topics that have been raised.

All the above interventions by the mediator should always be 'checked out' and confirmed by verbal or non-verbal validation. Should the party disagree, even slightly by signalling it in verbal or body posture, the mediator can immediately rectify it and tune in to the party's verbal and non-verbal communication.

Empathy

Communicating in an 'empathic' way is a fundamental skill in mediation. It is a key element which assists the mediator in establishing rapport and trust. It involves a projection of the mediator's own understanding into an understanding of what the party is saying and what is being expressed ('the music behind the words'). It entails understanding the experiences of the other person from that person's perspective.

Empathy and acceptance (see below) are mutually *in*clusive. Empathy is an acknowledgment and understanding of another person's position. In order to be 'empathic' the mediator must 'tune in', and *project* himself or herself into the personality and 'being' of the other, and seek to understand that personality or being – without judging, or evaluating, and certainly without challenging or confronting. Yet at the same time the mediator must 'tune out' or remain outside, and independent, in order to have a proper perspective upon the party's ambiguities and contradictions. If the mediator goes beyond merely an acknowledgment and understanding of the other's position, and begins simultaneously to *share* the feelings and emotions of the other party, he or she is demonstrating *sympathy*.

Sympathy involves one person sharing the emotions or feelings of another. When a mediator does this, he or she has lost his or her neutrality and independence. Empathy thus needs to be firmly distinguished from 'sympathy'. It requires *feeling with* the other person in a much more unified manner. Sympathy can jeopardize the mediator's neutrality and impartiality. By sympathizing with a party, the mediator may be seen as *agreeing with* the other person's point of view or being emotionally 'absorbed' in their position.

A number of metaphors have been used in an effort to illustrate the subtle differences between empathy and sympathy:

> If a driver drives into a ditch beside the road, and another passing motorist stops to help, that is empathy. If the passing motorist drives into the ditch alongside the first driver, that is sympathy.

In the above situation, the sympathetic driver is of no use to the motorist in the ditch, whereas the empathic driver is in a better position to help the other out of the predicament into which he has got himself. Similarly, the sympathetic mediator is of less effective use to the party than the empathic mediator. After all, no one wants their surgeon in floods of tears as he or she prepares to operate.

Acceptance and bracketing

The corollary of being non-judgmental is to embrace 'acceptance' – the art of acknowledging another person's stance or position, without judgment, challenge or contradiction, and accepting it as a 'valid' position to hold.

Acceptance is non-judgmentally taking on board the party's expressions *at their own valuation*. It means 'bracketing' or suspending one's own critical judgment, and accepting the party's position as valid and reasonable, from their point of view. By bracketing his or her own preconceived ideas, and suspending judgment in this way, the mediator allows the party to feel truly heard. The mediator should above all never appear to trivialize the problem.

Identifying themes

An important skill for the sensitive mediator is to 'identify themes'. These are recurring messages which parties impart, often quite unwittingly, and reveal issues which may be of particular importance to them. They may be manifested by the repetition of a single word, or it may be that the party repeatedly returns to a particular issue. In either case, it tends to signify that for the party expressing the word or raising the issue, there may be some hidden or greater significance, which might merit further exploration by the mediator.

Challenging/confronting/reality testing

There are a number of ways that a mediator can effectively 'challenge' a party in mediation. The mediator can:

- feed back contradictions, discrepancies and gaps between stated values and actions or words
- question the validity of a party's stance or expressed position
- suggest or invite a shift in approach or outlook
- reality test, by prompting a re-examination of assumptions
- invite the party to consider the catastrophic 'what if' scenario

Whichever method or style of challenge is adopted, as stated above, the mediator must always use challenges tentatively, carefully and with empathy. He or she must be acutely aware of the potentially confrontational impact and effect of such confrontation. Theoretically, the challenge is most appropriately used when tackling blockages which are preventing or impeding progress towards settlement. Providing they are used appropriately, challenges can be employed at any stage; but, if used at a stage when the mediator has not yet established a sufficient rapport or bond, the challenge can destroy the trust or respect invested by the party in the mediator.

Deconstructing/laddering/unpacking

This means 'staying with' the phenomenon which the party articulates. The mediator explores each issue or theme as it unfolds, as if 'deconstructing' a structure, or as if descending a ladder, or unpacking a parcel. Whichever issue the party is dealing with, whether apparently relevant or not, it will be interconnected with the party's emotions, value systems and self-concept, and can reveal the party's underlying agenda, their true intentions and motivations.

Body language

An important part of the mediator's role in the mediation process is the observation of body language. This provides a tool for further exploration of the parties' world-views.

Communication between the mediator and the party, like *all* communication, is not confined to verbal communication alone. It also includes 'pre-verbal' experiences, expressed in silences, in dialogues of mutual validations and in body language. Fritz Perls, the founder of 'Gestalt' therapy, was quoted by van de Riet *et al.* (1980: 27) as saying:

> The firmest ground of experience lies in the individual's awareness of bodily sensation.

Body language includes the phenomenon of 'gesture'. The word originates from the Latin *gestus*, meaning 'bodily action'. This carries information pertaining to thoughts and emotions.

J. M. Heaton (2002) says:

> A smile is a gesture. How do we learn the language of smiles? How does a child learn to recognize a smile? What do I have to know to see a smile as a smile and to know how to take it, how to respond to it?

Most gestures are recognized intuitively. It is not necessary to learn how to recognize a smile. Mediators do not require special tuition to learn to recognize body language and gestures. If they can focus on active listening and create an empathic relationship, they will be in a position to recognize the non-verbal signals and signs in which parties express their world-view. For instance, if a party in the caucus session recounts a sad event, but without a sad facial expression, the mediator may instantly feel that something is not genuine. He or she may possibly register this experience and perhaps use it at an appropriate point in the mediation.

Gestures may harbour knowledge which is not yet conscious. Thus the body can often express a person's world-view more accurately than verbal communication, which can frequently distort or trivialize what the person truly feels.

Emotions and body language go hand in hand; if emotions, verbal language and body language all reveal the party's world-view and, if the mediator has the capacity actively to listen to the verbal and non-verbal communications, he or she can soon acquire a valuable insight into their true motivations in the conflict and in the mediation.

The mediator's approach to the skills

It may be helpful to summarize some of the principles that an effective mediator should have in the forefront of his or her mind when employing the above-mentioned skills.

- The mediator should try to 'stay with' and focus on the facts or issues which the party puts forward. If the party veers off at a tangent, or appears to divert from a theme, or if they go 'all over the place', the mediator should not be distracted by his or her own agenda, and should avoid the temptation, possibly because of time restraints, to 'bring the party back on track'. Wherever the party starts from, or on whatever issue he or she focuses first, he or she is likely to come round eventually to the central issue or concern. Such meanderings are likely to be interconnected with that party's experiences, whether in life or in the dispute. This technique or skill, referred to as 'deconstructing' or 'laddering' or 'unpacking' (see above), enables the mediator to focus upon the true issues by 'staying with the phenomena'. If this focusing skill is appropriately used, it can be most effective in disclosing the party's true, hidden or underlying motivations, through their non-verbal and verbal language.
- Good mediation is about a process of 'mutual validation'. The mediator's intervention is always tentative, confirmed by verbal or non-verbal validation. Should the party disagree slightly by signalling it in verbal or body posture, the mediator immediately rectifies or redefines it and 'tunes in' to the party's verbal and non-verbal language.
- Mediators should seek to assume a *naive* approach in the dialogues with the parties. This will elicit a freer and more uninhibited dialogue, enabling the mediator more readily to tune in to the party's perceptual world. The mediator can thus accept phenomena as perceived without expressing preconceived judgments. According to Edmund Husserl (1859-1938) a Viennese philosopher, in order to understand the truth about

things, we need to direct our attention 'naively' to things themselves. So we tune into the party's perception without giving priority to any other thoughts, and simply record it. According to Spinelli (1989):

> In the act of simply recording in a descriptive manner what is consciously being experienced while avoiding any hierarchical assumptions, we are better able to examine an experience with far less prejudice and with a much greater degree of adequacy.

- As described above, a natural humanly shared predilection is the need for self-expression. The mediator who can provide the space and time for this inexorable human desire for free expression in a trusting environment will elicit from parties their true outlook on the dispute and be in a position to challenge them tacitly if appropriate.
- One of the mediator's initial stances, particularly in the caucus stage of mediation, should be that his or her function is to allow the parties to explore their ambivalences. This can be achieved simply by 'being with' the parties in a 'connected' relationship. This will enable the parties to move from an antagonistic position to one of a working alliance. As previously stated, the stance of the mediator is more important than his or her use of technique and skill: through this, the mediator changes from 'going through the motions of a mediation' to being an ordinary individual relating to the parties in a process of mutual exploration to resolve a problem.
- In training, the mediator should learn to accept feedback and constructive criticism without being defensive. Even if the feedback appears misconstrued or just 'wrong', it is important for the mediator to accept it at face value, for it represents the perception of the party on the receiving end. The mediator needs to take away from such feedback that whatever he or she may have intended, it was perceived in another way. The mediator can then process this feedback later. This is a vital tool in

mediation: mediators must be prepared to be criticized and attacked by the parties, and any attempt at defence by the mediator could be counterproductive.

By the proper deployment of the skills, and by adhering to these principles, mediators will gradually and instinctively become more tentative in their approach to their own interventions, and will be able to establish a greater trusting relationship with each of the contesting parties.

Part II

Practical and Legal Aspects of Mediation

4

What Is Mediation?

Introduction

The concept of introducing a 'third party neutral' to intercede in hostile and antagonistic bilateral relationships is not new. Throughout the ages, among tribal, cultural and ethnic groups across the world from Africa to Europe and Asia, from Central and Southern America to Japan, family or community elders have been asked to assist or 'conciliate' in conflict situations. China, during the successive imperial dynasties, adopted mediation as a primary method of resolving conflicts. Although under communism, China's concepts of mediation were changed to a more 'absolute' approach to right and wrong, today's Chinese society is still infused with Confucian virtues of compromise and traditional mediation techniques of dispute resolution.

Mediation is recorded as having been used in international conflicts in the nineteenth century, when for example, Great Britain mediated between Portugal and Brazil in 1825, and the Vatican (Pope Leo XII) between Germany and Spain over the Caroline Islands. Currently a great deal of international diplomacy can be characterized as mediation, and has been widely used in the Middle East, the Balkans, East Timor, as well as a large number of conflicts on the African continent. Some international conflict situations, however, such as that between the Israeli army and the Palestinians in the 'siege' of the Church of Nativity in Bethlehem in 2002, have been categorized as 'resolved by mediation'; whereas the negotiations were conducted by 'representatives' rather than a neutral intermediary, even though mediation techniques were extensively deployed.

A more formalized use of mediation began to emerge in the United States in the early twentieth century, although the ADR movement only truly became apparent there in the 1960s. It grew largely out of labour versus management conflicts, which resulted in extensive federal and state legislation: for example see the Federal Arbitration Act 1925; the National Labor Relations Act 1935, giving employees rights of collective bargaining; and the Taft–Hartley Act 1947, establishing the Federal Mediation and Conciliation Service. Interestingly, in present-day Hungary, where the Soviet legal system was dismantled in the post-independence years, the first legislative regulation of any form of ADR was introduced in 2000 with an act to govern mediation in health care disputes; but mediation was hitherto used in Hungary mainly in the field of labour relations, and is still in its infancy in the context of general commercial disputes.

In the UK, mediation has taken longer to materialize, and unfamiliarity and scepticism in relation to alternate dispute resolution processes are still widespread. Yet ADR, as an alternative to litigation, has grown out of an ever-increasing dissatisfaction with the legal process. Litigation is almost universally regarded as slow, cumbersome, costly and inadequate. Statistics show that between 60 per cent and 75 per cent of *successful* litigants in personal injury claims remained dissatisfied with the outcome (see Law Commission Survey 1994). Litigants often feel that:

- the award is too little
- the judgment comes too late bearing in mind the time taken to reach court
- the whole process was too costly
- the whole process was too time-consuming
- the litigation resulted in the end of a previously productive commercial relationship

Mediation was seen as the answer to many of these complaints, and is still seen by the government and the Lord Chancellor's Department (now the Department for Constitutional Affairs) as the means of ridding the courts of their inordinate backlog of cases, and easing the way towards rendering costly litigation a matter of last resort (see the Lord Chancellor's Discussion Paper on *Alternative Dispute Resolution*, November 1999).

Mediation can be used by the rich and by the poor. It can be used in multi-million pound international commercial disputes as readily as it can be invoked in minor neighbour disputes. It is swift, relatively cheap and has an extraordinary success rate of up to 85 per cent, depending upon which survey is taken: 85 per cent is taken from the Centre for Effective Dispute Resolution's press release August 1999; and 62 per cent from H. Genn's *Central London County Court Mediation*.

How mediation works in a legal environment

Mediation is to lawyers like sex is to teenagers: everyone seems to be talking about it; everyone seems to agree it's a good thing; but very few seem to have had any real experience of it. (Ian Walker of Russell Jones & Walker, at the CEDR Civil Justice Audit, April 2000)

The above quotation, regrettably, continues to be as pertinent as it was when first used. Misconceptions and misunderstandings about the nature and function of the mediation process continue to flourish – among lawyers as well as non-lawyers. But mediation has relevance to everybody who has occasion to deal with conflict – not just lawyers. It is both surprising and at the same time disappointing that so many people involved in conflict can know so little about so much. Many lawyers still believe mediation is a form of arbitration. Those members of the general public who have heard of the word think mediation is little more than a sophisticated mode of negotiation. Many believe that the mediator will in some way *judge* the issues between those in dispute. Others perceive it simply as an exercise in 'compromise reaching'. But it is really none of these.

Mediation is a form of Alternative Dispute Resolution (ADR) whereby a 'third party neutral' intervenes to *facilitate* and assist the disputing parties in reaching a mutually acceptable settlement. The mediator is neither a judge nor an arbitrator; he or she is not an adjudicator, nor someone who *imposes* a resolution or a settlement upon the parties. Instead, the mediator acts simply as a 'midwife, assisting in the labour and birth of a settlement'. The mediator will help by seeking to identify common aims and objectives, by re-opening lines of communication and by developing mutually acceptable proposals for settlement. In this way, the mediator can gently move the parties away from a preoccupation with their *rights and liabilities,* and nudge them towards an exploration of their *needs and interests* – the transition from a position of conflict to a position where they can form a 'working alliance'.

The essential characteristic of mediation has been described in this way (Riskin 1994):

> The central quality of mediation lies in its capacity to reorientate the parties toward each other, not by imposing rules on them, but by helping them to achieve a new and shared perception of their relationship, a perception that will redirect their attitudes toward one another.

Mediation has three fundamental and distinctive elements:

It is consensual: The parties in dispute decide whether an accord can be reached, and they control the nature and the terms of it. As the mediator does not impose any resolution or settlement or terms of agreement upon the parties, there is not the inevitable 'win/lose' situation that accompanies litigation or arbitration. The parties in this way have absolute control of the outcome: they have the power to reach a solution that may appear ostensibly unfair to one side, or they might even choose to ignore potentially relevant laws or regulations. Provided it is in their common interests, and the resolution is lawful, the parties are fully empowered to decide whether or not to agree and to sign.

> Mediation places the substantive outcome of the dispute within the control and determination of the parties themselves; it frees them from being subjected to the opinions and standards of outside higher authorities, whether legal or otherwise. Further, mediation not only allows the parties to set their own standards for an acceptable solution, it also requires them to search for solutions that are within their own capacity to effectuate . . . the parties set the standards and the parties themselves marshal the resources to resolve the dispute. (Alfini, Press, Sternlight, Stulberg 2001)

The parties are in this way removed from the coercive atmosphere of litigation, arbitration or adjudication. They are entitled to withdraw from the mediation process at any time, and are not bound by anything said or agreed until such time as they sign a settlement agreement. However, once the agreement is signed, the settlement becomes as legally binding and enforceable as if it were the subject of a contract or a court order.

The parties will also normally enter into a 'pre-mediation agreement' whereby they set out the ground rules and seek to govern certain constituent parts of the process – for example, the identity and expertise of the mediator(s); the persons who may attend the mediation; the duration and venue of the mediation, and so on.

It is private and confidential: The mediation is held not in public but in private, and one of the cornerstones of the process is that it is *confidential and 'without prejudice'*. Anything disclosed during the mediation is disclosed 'without prejudice' and cannot be used outside or in later proceedings should the parties fail to reach agreement. Moreover, any information shared by one party with the mediator will be treated in confidence and the mediator must not pass it on to the other party without specific permission to do so.

It focuses not on 'rights and liabilities', but on 'needs and interests': The reason for the failure of many lengthy and protracted negotiations is that the parties all too readily fall into and get 'bogged down' in entrenched positions, and are unable to overcome the impasse that results. These entrenched positions derive from a 'rights culture' – a preoccupation with the *rights and liabilities* of the past:

> We insist upon receiving this because it is our *entitlement* – we demand that because it is your *obligation* to provide us with it.

Unlike litigation, which determines 'what happened in the past, why it happened and whose fault it was', mediation looks to the future and encourages parties to re-evaluate their aims and objectives in the dispute by re-examining their current and their future *needs and interests*:

> Although we may be entitled to this, do we *really need* it? Can we live without it?

or

> Even if we are obliged to provide you with this, it may be in our mutual *interests* to explore other options and to provide you with this in another form, or something else altogether.

Mediation as only one form of ADR

Alternative Dispute Resolution – but alternative to what? ADR is the generic term for an entire spectrum of processes which provide means of resolving disputes, *alternative to conventional court litigation*. There are a number of recognized important forms of ADR, with which this book is not concerned. However, it may be important to be aware of them:

Adjudication
A neutral third party is nominated by mutual agreement between the parties to adjudicate the dispute between them; but this is distinguished from mediation by the fact that the adjudicator is

there to render a *binding* decision, often after considering the evidence and/or arguments. Because this, like Arbitration, involves no negotiation in the process, and adopts an imposed solution creating a 'win-lose' outcome, it is considered by many to be outside the true scope of ADR.

Conciliation

A neutral third party is nominated to assist the parties in resolving issues, but again it is distinguished from mediation by the fact that the conciliator's role may be more 'interventionist' and includes that of recommending solutions and actively narrowing the issues.

Early Neutral Evaluation (ENE)

This usually occurs within the litigation process after proceedings have been issued. It involves the parties consensually submitting their dispute to a third party neutral nominated by them to evaluate their respective prospects of success if the matter were to proceed to court. The opinion of the evaluator is not binding, but is intended to encourage settlement.

Expert Evaluation

This is similar to Early Neutral Evaluation (above) but is used in disputes of a more technical or scientific nature, where the third party neutral is recognized as an expert in the field of the dispute.

Expert Determination

This is again similar to ENE and Expert Evaluation, in that it is the consensual nomination of an expert neutral third party, but the parties have agreed that the expert's opinion will be binding upon the parties, and will determine the dispute.

Judicial Appraisal

The parties can agree to submit the entirety of their dispute – or restricted to a single issue – to a senior lawyer, usually a retired judge or QC, for appraisal of the respective merits of each party's case. It is again non-binding, but has the advantage of being an authoritative opinion, which can form the basis of an agreement or settlement.

Facilitative versus evaluative mediation

There are two distinct models or styles of conventional mediation: 'facilitative' and 'evaluative'. The facilitative form of mediation has been described as 'minimalist' (Palmer and Roberts 1988) or 'non-interventionist' (Boulle and Nesic 2001), and is confined to assisting the parties to communicate and negotiate with each other in order to reach a measure of accord. Evaluative mediation tends to be more 'directive and interventionist', in that the mediator may provide the parties with an evaluation of the respective merits and demerits, and strengths and weaknesses of the parties' cases.

Leonard Riskin (1994) put it this way:

The evaluative mediator assumes that the participants want and need the mediator to provide some direction as to the appropriate grounds for settlement – based on law, industry practice or technology. She [*sic*] also assumes that the mediator is qualified to give such direction by virtue of her experience, training and objectivity. The facilitative mediator assumes the parties are intelligent, able to work with their counterparts, and capable of understanding their situations better than either their lawyers or the mediator. For these reasons, the facilitative mediator assumes that his [*sic*] principal mission is to enhance and clarify communications between the parties in order to help them decide what to do.

There are those who say that evaluation forms an important part of every mediation process. Indeed, where the mediator has *particular* authority or great weight of experience well exceeding that of the parties at the mediation, he or she can often deploy the weight of his or her influence to good effect. But where the mediator is more 'peer-based' (Boulle and Nesic 2001), coming from the parties' peer group, attempts at evaluation can frequently be interpreted as an exercise in 'head-bashing'.

Those who choose an evaluative mediator, or a mediator who is an expert in the particular field of the dispute, may be seen as implicitly assenting to his or her greater expertise or competence. They tend to look to him or her to provide direction for resolution, based upon a particular knowledge and expertise. The mediator's neutrality is thus often put to the test:

> You're a specialist, you know we are right, persuade the other side to . . .'

There will be a corresponding propensity on the part of the evaluative or specialist mediator to offer professional advice or give an opinion, creating a problematic mix of roles: mediator/professional adviser.

Evaluative mediation can also very easily descend into 'trashing and bashing' (Alfini 1991). The 'trashing mediator' spends much of the private caucus sessions with each party 'trashing' their case, pointing out the inherent weaknesses, or simply 'tearing it apart'. He or she will also seek to obtain as much 'ammunition' and information from that party to take across to the other party in caucus, in order to be in a position to 'trash' their opposing case with equal vigour. Frequently, the mediator employing a 'trashing' technique will draw upon his or her own experiences, whether as a veteran litigator, advocate or judge, and give a predictive opinion, based upon that experience, as to the outcome if the matter were to proceed to court. As stated above, if such opinion emanates from a mediator of considerable stature, authority or expertise, it can cause the parties seriously to re-evaluate their prospects of success and create a more 'realistic' approach to settlement. However, in some jurisdictions, such techniques are proscribed: for example, in the *Florida Rules for Court Appointed Mediators (2000)*, Rule 10.370 states:

the Mediator shall not offer a personal or professional opinion as to how the court will resolve the dispute.

The more purist view of mediation is that evaluation is the antithesis of facilitation – it discourages *self*-evaluation, prevents self-determination, promotes positioning, results in polarization and encourages parties to focus on their rights and liabilities rather than their interests and needs. An effective mediator, even when 'reality testing', encourages the parties to question their own assumptions, re-evaluate their own positions, re-orientate their attitudes towards each other, focus on their real interests and thereby expand their options for settlement. Thus in this book, it is proposed that mediation should be restricted to a 'facilitative' form, and that the mediator, in most cases, should not enter the arena to 'evaluate' the respective parties' cases. At the very least,

> evaluations, especially of a predictive nature, generally should be resorted to only after other more facilitative measures have failed to break the impasse. (Weckstein 1997)

Once the mediator embarks upon evaluating the claims, he or she surrenders his or her neutrality, and will no longer be able properly to continue to act as an impartial neutral.

5

Negotiate or Mediate?

Parties turning to mediation will almost inevitably have gone through a period of negotiation, for negotiation constitutes a primary form of dispute resolution. Lawyers will resolve a large percentage of their case-load by negotiated agreements, hence the instinctive response of a lawyer when mediation is suggested is:

> Why do we need a mediator? I am an experienced negotiator, I spend every day negotiating settlements. What can a mediator bring to this dispute that I as an experienced negotiator cannot?

Positional bargaining

The answer to the above rhetorical question is this: mediation inevitably involves elements of negotiation, but the nature and type of negotiation is wholly different to that normally conducted by lawyers in their everyday practices. The negotiation used in mediation has been termed *principled* negotiation, whereas the type of negotiation adopted by lawyers is often referred to as *positional* or *strategic*.

The distinction between *principled* and *positional* negotiation was first espoused by Roger Fisher and William Ury in 1981 in the revolutionary work, *Getting to Yes*, where they urged negotiators to:

separate the people from the problem, focus on interests rather than positions, invent options for mutual gain, and insist on using objective criteria.

'Rottweiler or poodle' as negotiator?

The positional nature of the bargaining process conducted by lawyers is dictated by the very nature of their own position, as *champions* for their clients. Invariably when the parties have exhausted all attempts at resolving the problem directly between themselves, they feel they have no alternative but to 'now place the matter in the hands of our lawyers'. This may frequently be accompanied by the sentiment: 'and *my* lawyers will have you for breakfast'. Similarly, lawyers believe that when their clients come to them, they want action: they want to see their claim pursued with vigour and aggression, or they want to see the other side's claim defended with equal hostility and ferocity. In other words, lawyers frequently have a perception that their clients want them to act as rottweilers, rather than poodles.

And so when lawyers enter into negotiations they do so rather as white knights or gladiators, with instructions not just to do the best they can, but to utterly destroy the opposition. The lawyers in turn will see their purpose as not simply to achieve a reasonable settlement but to secure an outright conquest. The effect of this upon the strategies adopted by negotiators can readily be seen. Take the following example:

> Party A and Party B are in dispute over the amount of damages payable in respect of a delivery of faulty goods. Party A would be willing to pay £40,000. In commencing negotiations, however, his solicitor does not offer £40,000, but opens the bargaining process by offering £20,000. Party B on the other hand would be willing to accept £40,000, but his solicitor does not indicate a willingness to accept £40,000. He responds by demanding £60,000. The parties thus start the negotiations with £40,000 between them, whereas they might have been prepared to settle immediately at £40,000.

The motivating factor for each solicitor in putting forward an 'extreme' offer is the fact that they are involved in *representative bargaining*, acting as *champions* for their clients. They would like to achieve a result that is *better* than the client expected; this they believe will earn them respect, gratitude and admiration – and further work.

Competitive bargaining has the purpose of maximising the competitive bargainer's gain over the gain of those with whom he negotiates. He is in effect trying to 'come out ahead of', or 'do better than', all other parties in the negotiation. For this reason we sometimes refer to this competitive bargaining strategy as a 'domination' strategy, meaning that the competitive bargainer tends to treat negotiations as a kind of contest to win. (Goodpaster 1996)

What follows such 'positional bargaining' is a process of justification, where the negotiator must substantiate the level of offer or demand made, and provide a reasonable rationale for it, both on a factual basis and in legal terms.

'My client's claim is worth £60,000 because: a) ..., b)..., c)...', etc.
'My client is not prepared to pay more than £20,000 because: x)..., y)..., z)...', etc.

This will inevitably involve posturing, bluff and counter-bluff, deception and the withholding of potent information which might be seen as damaging the case.

The competitive negotiator adopts a risky strategy which involves the taking of firm almost extreme positions, making few and small concessions, and withholding information that may be useful to the other party. The intention and hoped-for effect behind this basic strategy is to persuade the other party that it must make concessions if it is to get an agreement. In addition to this basic strategy, the competitive negotiator may also use various ploys and tactics aimed at pressurising, unsettling, unbalancing, or even misleading the other party to secure an agreement with its demands ... the competitive negotiator wants to persuade the other side about the firmness of the negotiator's own *asserted* bottom line. The competitive negotiator works to convince the other party that it will settle at some point that is higher or lower than its actual unrevealed bottom line. Taking a firm position and conceding little will incline the other party to think the competitor has little to give. Thus if there is to be a deal, then the other party must give or concede more. (ibid. 1996)

Clients can exacerbate the situation – whether consciously or subconsciously – by disguising or leaving unspoken their under-lying motivations, and concealing even from their 'representative negotiators' their true aspirations or objectives. They tell their lawyers what they think their lawyers wish to hear. The adverse affect of all these bargaining strategies is often further aggravated because such negotiation techniques inescapably involve high-lighting the *differences* between the parties, rather than pointing out their *common* interests.

Characteristics of negotiation

Many lawyers believe that as a result of their considerable experi-ence in negotiation, they are 'natural born mediators'. However, negotiators who are not trained in 'principled negotiation' or the art of mediation will have the further disadvantage of

being people first, who get angry, depressed, fearful, hostile, frustrated and offended. They have egos that are easily threa-tened. They see the world from their own personal vantage point, and they frequently confuse perceptions with reality. They routinely fail to interpret what you say in the way that you intend, and do not mean what you understand them to say. (adapted from Condlin 1992)

Conversely, many people in Western society have an aversion to bargaining, or negotiating. They will pay the requested price in any bazaar or market even where some 'haggling' and 'horse-trading' is expressly expected. These personalities will find strategic negotiating a very uncomfortable process.

Hostility between negotiators will also hamper the progress towards agreement. For it is much easier to negotiate with friends whom you trust and respect, than with enemies whom you distrust and hold in contempt.

Communication between clients is forbidden

'How dare your client speak to mine!'

The unfortunate aspect of litigation culture in the UK is that once the matter is in the hands of the lawyers, all direct communication between the parties themselves is expressly forbidden. Even in matrimonial or family disputes, where the parties still reside under the same roof, solicitors have been known to write to the spouse's solicitor, urging them to remind their client that 'now the matter is in the hands of the respective solicitors, all direct communications between the clients are strictly prohibited, and any negotiations in future should be conducted exclusively through the lawyers and not directly between the parties'.

This 'How dare your client speak to mine' attitude on the part of UK solicitors means that the parties are left entirely in the hands of their negotiating representatives, and can only hope that they prove to have the personality and the skill to bring about an amicable settlement.

'Chinese whispers'

A further drawback of parties being forbidden to communicate other than through their solicitors is the 'Chinese whispers' syndrome. Most negotiations will be conducted 'at arm's length' by the solicitors through offers and counter-offers made in writing, and relayed in writing to the respective clients. The parties thus learn of the other side's stance by a letter arriving on their desk or their doormat. A reasonable stance or proposal communicated to a party's lawyer can readily become distorted in its onward communication to the other party. Take the following example:

> Party A writes to his solicitor: 'I would very much like to pay my ex-wife more than I am currently paying, but I simply and genuinely cannot afford it.'
>
> Party A's solicitor informs Party B's solicitor: 'My client simply cannot pay your client any more, and if your client persists in this claim, we will have no alternative but to go to court.'
>
> Party B's solicitor writes to his client: 'Your ex-husband has indicated that he is not prepared to pay you a penny more, and that he would rather see you in court.'

In these ways, the parties become more deeply and more firmly entrenched in their opposing adversarial and confrontational positions.

Litigator's loss of objectivity
Experienced litigators can frequently be hampered in their negotiations by a natural tendency to lose their objectivity as their client's case progresses towards trial.

> Many successful litigators are individuals who exhibit what Eric Hoffer has described as 'true believer' personalities (E. Hoffer, *The True Believer*, Harper & Row, 1951). As they become prepared for trial, they no longer entertain uncertainties, concerning the right of their clients to prevail. Whilst this phenomenon may increase their capacity to present clients' cases forcefully ... it usually diminishes their ability to achieve negotiated resolutions. As these individuals become more convinced of the certainty of their impending 'victories', they lose all perspective regarding the objective strengths and weaknesses of their cases. (Craver 2001)

Splitting the difference
A frequent outcome of negotiations, particularly where positional

bargaining has been widely employed, is that the parties are faced with the prospect of either resigning themselves to the fact that settlement will not be achieved, or alternatively making significant mutual concessions. Such mutual concessions are often little more than face-saving devices, where the parties are persuaded to make simultaneous gestures of movement. This often takes the form of 'splitting the difference (down the middle)' and settling at a mid-point figure. Such form of compromise is frequently unsatisfactory, because:

- each party feels that the mid-point was achieved by their having made more concessions than the other party
- it leaves each party feeling they were obliged to give up a part of their claim which they otherwise might have secured
- each party leaves feeling that they have 'lost' and that the negotiations were not truly successful
- each party is left wondering whether they might have achieved more had they pursued their claim further and not compromised so soon

Mediation and negotiation compared

Mediation frequently succeeds where negotiations have failed. Mediation overcomes many of the foregoing problems arising out of negotiation and negotiated settlements. The negotiations are carried out face-to-face or in close proximity with the opposing parties, and not at arm's length, as described above. The parties can be truly 'heard', thus overcoming some of the emotional and psychological barriers discussed in other chapters in this book; and both parties are in a position to control their own settlement. The skilled mediator will focus upon *needs* and *interests* – not *rights* and *liabilities*, thereby encouraging an ethos of cooperation between the parties. This enables parties to get closer to the '*win-win*' settlement they desire, where they can feel they have achieved a 'good' outcome, or, perhaps more importantly, at least an outcome that is 'good enough' for their true purposes.

6

What Actually Happens at a 'Legal' Mediation?

The following is an outline of the format of a typical UK model of 'legal' mediation, generally accepted throughout this country in non-family mediation. Variations of this format are used in family mediation and also adopted in some European countries.

Mediation opening

Effecting the introductions
There are no prescribed rules as to where a mediation should take place. It will generally be conducted at one or other of the parties' lawyers' offices. In some court-annexed mediation, the process takes place on court premises after court sitting hours.

The mediation usually commences with all parties together in one room, invariably around a table. The mediator should effect the introductions, seeking to create an informal atmosphere – and no doubt hoping for an opportunity to break the ice. Inane small talk can often be irritating, or sometimes even offensive:

'What awful weather, isn't it! It always seems to rain when I am mediating.'

'Did you have a good journey here – or were there "leaves on the track" again?'

On the other hand, some light-hearted humour, sensitively delivered, can be effective in breaking the ice and enabling parties to relax.

The manner in which people like to be addressed can be important, and the option of whether or not to use or discard titles (for example: Dr ..., Major ..., Lord ..., Sir ..) or first names and surnames should be clearly established. The easiest way, perhaps, is for the mediator to start by introducing himself:

'I am John Smith, and I am happy if you would call me John throughout this mediation.'

Hopefully the others will follow suit. But there are no hard and fast rules. In some instances the parties have never been on first-name terms and suddenly to start referring to each other by their first names will feel unnatural, false and forced. On the other hand, it may prove to be just what is required to break down pre-existing formal barriers. As in most aspects of mediation, it will be a matter of judgment for the mediator. In any event, any faux pas or indiscretion needs to be carefully avoided, as for instance:

'May I call you by your Christian name?'

when the person being addressed may not be a Christian and might take offence.

Seating
Throughout the initial stages of the mediation the mediator's prime objective is to create a 'safe environment' in which the parties will feel suitably comfortable and secure. The atmosphere must in every respect be conducive to reaching an amicable settlement. Any situation or incident at this early stage that causes tension, embarrassment or discomfort can disrupt the process and initiate an unfortunate climate for the start to the proceedings.

The mediator will thus need to consider and to arrange the seating so that none of the parties feels unduly ill at ease. There are entire chapters in books and treatises on mediation analysing the most appropriate and effective seating arrangements, for these can often be underestimated. The most readily available seating is around a rectangular or square table: here there is a natural temptation to place the parties on opposite sides, and the mediator at one end between them. However, this can tend to reinforce the confrontational stance of the two sides. It can also create an impression that the mediator is a judge or arbitrator whose role it is to decide between the two sides and find in favour of one or other. On the other hand, if the parties are seated on the same side of the table, care must be taken so as not to place them unduly close to each other, as the discomfort or embarrassment that this may create can be an impediment to the safe environment that an effective mediator is trying to create. Similarly, if the mediator is not seated equidistant from both parties, a sense of partiality can unwittingly be imparted to the persons further away. A round table may be ideal, albeit again with the parties neither opposite nor too close to each other; or a square table with the parties around one corner and the mediator on the opposite side (Korda 1975).

The mediator may also need to be sensitive to hierarchies: the mediation may be attended by the party, or representatives of the party such as the Chief Executive, or the Sales Director, or the Accountant, together with the lawyer, the lawyer's assistant, the Expert Witness, the wife or husband, the uncle and aunt, the friend, etc. If for example, the mediator seats the lawyer next to the mediator, with the party on the other side of the lawyer, there is an immediate impression created that the mediator wishes to hear *firstly* from the lawyer rather than the client. By placing the client closest to the mediator and the lawyer a little further away, the mediator can reinforce the view that the client party is the most important person and the lawyer is simply there to provide advice and assistance. The attenders will have a hierarchy among themselves, which they may wish to retain – or relinquish, and so similar considerations may apply to the experts, accountants, relatives and other attenders.

The mediator's opening address

Generally
The mediator's opening statement can be vitally important in setting the right tone for the remainder of the sessions. An articulate and informative opening delivered in a calming and reassuring manner will quickly convey a sense of the mediator's skill and competence. The mediator's principal task is to build trust and create a rapport with the parties, and the opening statement is an excellent first opportunity. The mediator should use the statement to establish his or her credibility and impartiality, and to put the parties at ease. If the parties have had no previous experience of the particular mediator, there will almost certainly be some element of anxiety on the part of each side as to whether the mediator will prove to be truly impartial, really effective and suitably competent. If the mediator, through the opening address, can create confidence and trust in him or herself as mediator, as well as in the mediation process, the parties will be less reticent, and may find the experience more 'inviting' and conducive to openness and candour. The mediator should thus also demonstrate a certain level of control, for control over the process tends to generate confidence as well as greater discussion, and allows greater freedom to the parties to control the outcome (*see* Slaikeu 1996; and Brunet and Craver 1997).

Aims of the process and role of the mediator
The mediator will outline the aims of the process and the mediator's role in it. It remains surprising how many parties attending mediations, whether experienced lawyers or simply members of the public, are not aware of how mediation works. So it will be necessary for the mediator to state the purpose of the process and how it works. The mediator will outline and emphasize that his or her function is that of a neutral facilitator and *not* an adjudicator or arbitrator. Again, by emphasizing both the voluntary and the confidential nature of the process – that the parties may leave at

any stage if they wish, and that nothing said in the mediation can be used or repeated outside – the mediator will help to create that secure environment so necessary for successful mediations.

Procedure

The mediator will outline the procedure, detailing the way in which joint sessions and private 'caucus' sessions will be used. This should include, in order to avoid creating offence or suspicion, the order in which parties speak or are seen in the caucus sessions. The mediator should be sensitive to the possibility that his or her choice as to which party speaks or is seen or spoken to first, may be interpreted as indications of partiality.

Timing

It may also be prudent to deal with the issue of timing: to set out the fact that the mediator will try to ensure that the amount of time each party will be allowed in caucus is the same, but that this may not be possible on every occasion. The mediator should in any event emphasize that each party will have an *equal opportunity* rather than *equal time*. This will pre-empt 'clock watching' while the mediator is with the other side, and will again reduce concerns about partiality.

It may also be prudent to ensure that the parties are in agreement as to the duration of the mediation. It is not conducive to settlement – and can be most infuriating to parties as well as the mediator – if one party needs to leave at a certain point in the sessions, whereas the other party is 'willing to stay all night if necessary'.

The ground rules

These will need to be set out: that it is a voluntary process with each party free to leave if they wish; that it is entirely confidential and everything is deemed to be 'without prejudice'. The importance of the mediator explaining the confidentiality of the process cannot be overemphasized. Confidentiality is a crucial element of mediation: it encourages participants to speak openly and with candour. The greater the disclosure by the parties of their real concerns, fears, interests, needs and aspirations, the greater the prospect of the mediator being able successfully to facilitate a settlement. If participants were to have the slightest hesitation as to whether their disclosures to the mediator would remain in confidence, and thus whether they could be used against them in later proceedings, the parties would not speak openly and little progress could be made.

Note-taking

There are, curiously, wide-ranging views about the propriety of note-taking during the mediation, whether on the part of the mediator or by the parties and their advisers. Note-taking can impinge upon the issue of confidentiality, as well as being a distraction. If the parties see the mediator taking notes, they may become overly concerned as to what is being noted:

> Why did the mediator note this? Does he consider it important? Is he going to relay it to the other side? Why did he not make a note of the other point I made?

Similarly, there may be an undue temptation on the part of one or other persons present to see what the mediator has written. Perhaps more importantly, excessive note-taking by the mediator can unduly disrupt the eye contact that can be so important in establishing rapport. On the other hand, note-taking may assist both the mediator and the parties to remember issues they may wish to raise later, and can encourage them to listen to new information without needing to interrupt each other (Alfini *et al.* 2001).

Checking 'authority to settle'

The parties at the mediation frequently consist of 'representatives' of another organization or institution – whether employees, directors, partners or spouses. The mediator will need to ascertain that the representatives have the authority to conclude the process by signing the agreement if a settlement is reached. Too many mediations flounder at the final stage, when one of the parties 'disappears' in order to check with his or her board, or executive, or partner, or spouse, or superiors, or the insurers, as to whether the proposed settlement is acceptable.

Parties' opening statements

Each party, and/or their legal advisor, makes a short opening statement, without interruption, setting out the main points of their case. This is a vital element of the mediation and its effect should not be underestimated. It can set the tone for the entire proceedings that follow. Where the dispute has hitherto been conducted by correspondence, it may well be the first time that the parties meet face-to-face; it will probably be the first time that one party has an opportunity to hear the other side's story first hand, rather than sifted, repeated and interpreted by a number of inter-mediaries. It will invariably be the first time, for example, that one party's insurer or other decision-maker comes face to face with the other party. And sometimes it is the first opportunity to see the other side's lawyers 'in action'; this can often be a salutary experi-ence, as each party will undoubtedly have had a mental image of the other side's lawyers, as inhuman and incompetent and perhaps to see that they are 'human', and doing just as good a job – if not better – than their own lawyers, can occasionally help to move the dispute forward. For these reasons, the opening statements can be a most therapeutic constituent of the process, and consequently the parties should use it to good advantage.

> When emotionally charged controversies and relationships are involved, cathartic 'venting' may permit the dissipation of strong feelings that might preclude realistic consideration of possible solutions. The mediator should allow the requisite venting in an environment that is likely to minimise the crea-tion of unproductive animosity. (Brunet and Craver 1997)

The above quotation represents a slightly differing view to those expressed in the bulk of this book. 'Cathartic venting' would require a critical analysis of its meaning, and 'unproductive animosity' is diametrically opposed to the concept of the positive aspects of emotions such as anger, as outlined throughout this work. Nevertheless, the quotation serves to demonstrate a typical but conventional approach of many mediators towards the mediation process.

Too frequently, lawyers are asked to furnish their party's opening address and use the occasion simply to regurgitate, ostensibly for the mediator's benefit, a series of legal submissions. This merely demonstrates that the party has misunderstood the role and function of the mediator, mistaking him or her for an arbitrator, and only serves to irritate the other side:

'Oh no, not those old chestnuts again – we've heard all this before!'

Rather, the parties should be encouraged to give their statements themselves, setting out a more personal perspective of the dispute, augmented if necessary by their lawyers. This is 'their day in court' and it is their chance to be truly heard and to convey the extent and depth of their feelings – 'to tell it from the heart':

'this is what you have done to me'
'this is how your clients have affected my entire life/business'
'this is why we cannot accept anything less'
'this is why we cannot pay you any more'

It is also the mediator's first real opportunity to listen out for and to identify the true issues, the underlying motivations and hidden agendas that may exist but have hitherto not been brought to the surface by either party. Furthermore, it is equally the mediator's first opportunity to deploy all the skills of active listening – maintaining eye contact, nodding, expressing words of empathy and so on – so as to help build confidence and trust.

Private caucus session

'Mediators do it in separate rooms'

At the conclusion of the opening statements, the parties will generally (in the UK model of mediation) separate for the separate 'caucus' sessions into their respective rooms. This simply means the private individual session where the mediator sees each party privately and in confidence on their own. If there is a room allocated for the mediation itself, the mediator may invite each party to come to that room for the private caucus sessions. More usually, however, the mediator will visit the parties in their respective rooms. The format of the foregoing will obviously depend upon the venue, the number of parties, whether the mediator is acting alone or with a co-mediator, and the facilities available in each room.

The private caucus session is where the mediator communicates directly and in confidence with each party in turn. The caucus is not universally used in mediation. For example, it is employed rarely in family mediation, where most of the sessions are conducted with the parties jointly. Similarly, in some American and many European models of mediation, the caucus is almost never used at all.

For the purposes of the model of mediation discussed in this book, the caucus is the most crucial phase of mediation. This is the exploratory stage, where each party is encouraged to speak more openly about issues and potential options for settlement than they would if in the presence of the other party. The mediator, using all the skills and techniques dealt with in a later chapter, will attempt to:

- explore and identify the core issues of the dispute
- investigate the hidden features lying behind and beneath those issues
- ascertain the true underlying needs, interests and objectives of the respective parties
- skilfully and delicately move the parties from their entrenched

positions to a position where they re-evaluate their aims, objectives and aspirations

- gently challenge assumptions, and 'test the reality' of the party's case or proposition
- examine the options for settlement

The more 'high-context' information the mediator is able to extract from and share with the parties, the greater are the prospects of finding common ground for a settlement. Confidentiality is the cornerstone of the caucus phase and the private caucus session allows the parties to evaluate the effect of the options for settlement without the pressures and constraints of a joint session. Similarly the mediator is able to challenge and 'reality test' in a way that would be impossible if the other side were present.

It is important that an effective mediator gives repeated reminders of the confidentiality of the caucus session, and that nothing revealed will be passed on to the other party unless specific permission is given. This helps to maintain trust and encourages openness. The mediator's aim throughout is to maintain neutrality, establish rapport and gain trust.

Joint session

The separate caucus sessions will normally continue until such time as the mediator feels it appropriate to bring the parties back together. The question as to whether, and if so when, the mediator should bring the parties back together for a joint session is largely a matter of judgment, either for the mediator alone, or with the input of the other parties. It can also be a matter of style: those who adopt the model of mediation in which caucuses are rarely used, will prefer to conduct as much of the mediation in joint session as possible. They believe that joint sessions give greater opportunity for the parties to communicate directly with each other, and that caucuses break the flow of joint communication. Similarly, others argue that by calling for a caucus immediately following the joint statements, or too soon, or too often, or not allowing sufficient joint sessions,

> the mediator has not provided the parties with the opportunity to negotiate for themselves, and has thereby not fostered joint problem-solving. (Alfini *et al.* 2001)

Joint sessions can effectively be used when the parties have reached a sufficient accord in principle, so as to justify bringing them together to shape the finer points of the settlement. Whether the parties have in fact reached such a stage may in itself be a delicate judgment call. Take the following example:

> The mediator, in the caucus sessions, has secured a measure of agreement between the parties: they have agreed to settle on the basis of a 'modest' payment of money together with an apology. Triumphantly the mediator brings the parties together for a final joint session to 'hammer out' a settlement agreement. They soon discover, however, that what one party regarded as appropriate terms of an apology were totally different to those envisaged by the other, and that their views as to the size of a 'modest payment' were equally dissimilar. The mediator finds himself listening to insults hurled across the table:
>
> > 'You call that a "modest sum"? I call it downright miserly! And if you think that is an acceptable apology then think again!'

In a brief moment, all the effort and work of the last few hours is lost. On the other hand, if the mediator allows him or herself to be used as a 'shuttle diplomat' for too long, or merely as a courier for the conveyance of offers and counter-offers, the momentum of movement towards settlement can be impeded.

Settlement agreement

Once a true settlement is reached, the step that transforms the mediation from a voluntary non-binding process into a fully binding accord is the signing of a settlement agreement. The parties will need to create a document which they can each sign to signify their acceptance to being bound. A 'Heads of Agreement' document will usually be drafted immediately, either by the parties themselves or by the lawyers if they are present, or by the mediator. It needs to be sufficiently clear and unambiguous so as to 'make it stick', and be a reliable record of the accord reached so as to render the signatures obtained upon it of legal value.

The only matter then remaining is to decide who buys the champagne!

7

Embarking upon Mediation

This chapter seeks to outline the more 'legalistic' criteria that the parties to a dispute may need to consider when embarking upon mediation within a litigation environment.

The timing for mediation

Although nearly all disputes are amenable to mediation, there will be stages within the conflict when mediation may not be appropriate. At the outset of serious disagreements leading to potential litigation, parties may not be too sympathetic to the idea of mediation. They will very often be in a belligerent state. They may feel incensed and irate. They may feel wounded and dishonoured. They may want vindication and retribution, preferably in the form of a public humiliation of the other party by the judge in open court. What they will be looking for perhaps, is an aggressive lawyer, a 'rottweiler', who will pursue or defend their claim with vigour and passion. In these circumstances, they are less likely to be receptive to the idea of a 'softly, softly' approach as presented by mediation.

More importantly perhaps, the parties may not be armed with sufficient information, whether about their own position or about that of the other side, with which to enter into meaningful settlement negotiations. For instance, in a Personal Injury or Clinical

Negligence dispute, the claimant may not have a clear picture at the outset of the full extent of the injuries: they may not know the precise condition from which they are suffering, the exact cause of it and most importantly the prognosis. In other disputes, the full terms of a contract may not yet be ascertained, or technical reports, product specifications, safety records or design histories, etc. may not be available. In these circumstances, attempts at early settlement could prove premature, and so it may be advisable to delay mediation until all this information is available.

The purists in mediation will argue that all the foregoing information simply tends to concentrate the parties' minds on rights and liabilities, making them dwell on the past, and encouraging endless examination of 'who, what, and why'. The purists will contend that the parties should rather be focusing on needs and interests, and exploring constructive ways forward through mediation. There is undoubtedly force in this argument, and a balance will need to be carefully drawn between entering into the mediation process prematurely, and waiting too long in the information-gathering stage.

There may be disputes which, though amenable to mediation, are nevertheless not appropriate for resolution outside the courts. The following are some examples:

- where a dispute involves a matter of public policy
- where a Court ruling is required in relation to matters of safety or procedure
- where a Court ruling is necessary to establish proprietary rights
- where a precedent is required in interpretation of the law
- where an exemplary award of damages is needed

It may be difficult – but not impossible – to mediate in cases where there is no genuine desire to settle on the part of one or more of the parties. If one party simply wishes to punish the other, or to see the other humiliated or crushed, even the most skilful and effective mediator may encounter difficulties in facilitating a settlement. It is perhaps for these reasons that family mediation has not had as great a success rate as the government, the lawyers and the parties would wish. Where one spouse or partner simply wants to 'beat the other party over the head with the heaviest sharpest implement on which they can lay their hands', the gentle non-confrontational approach of mediation is hardly likely to satisfy their requirements.

Finally, the question arises as to whether parties can refuse to participate in mediation and at the same time be regarded – by the courts and elsewhere – as acting *reasonably*. The permissible reasons for refusing to mediate have been very severely restricted by certain recent decisions of the English courts. In the case of *Cowl & Ors v Plymouth City Council* [2002] 1 WLR 803, the claimants were the occupants of a residential care home run by Plymouth City Council and were seeking in the Courts to challenge the local authority's decision to close the home. When giving his judgment, Lord Justice Woolf made the following crucial comments:

> We do not single out either side's lawyers for particular criticism. What followed was due to the unfortunate culture in litigation of this nature of over-judicialising the processes which are involved. It is indeed unfortunate that, that process having started, instead of the parties focussing on the future they insisted on arguing about what had occurred in the past. So far as the claimants were concerned, that was of no value since Plymouth were prepared, as they ultimately made clear was their position, to re-consider the whole issue. Without the need for the vast costs which must have been incurred in this case already being incurred, the parties should have been able to come to a sensible conclusion as to how to dispose the issues which divided them. If they could not do this without help, then an independent mediator should have been recruited to assist. That would have been a far cheaper course to adopt. Today sufficient should be known about ADR to make the failure to adopt it, in particular when public money is involved, indefensible.

Shortly after this case was heard, a further landmark decision was made in January 2002, when the Court of Appeal sent a shiver down the spines of many litigators, by refusing to award costs in favour of a *successful* litigant, on the grounds that they had *unreasonably* refused to participate in mediation. The case was *Dunnett v Railtrack* (2002) 1 WLR 2434 and the brief facts were as follows:

The claimant had kept horses in a field adjoining a railway line, owned and controlled by Railtrack PLC. A gate providing access to the line fell into disrepair and was replaced by Railtrack with a metal gate, which did not shut automatically but had to be specifically closed. On an occasion when the gate had been left open, the horses escaped onto the line and were hit by a train. The Claimant found the horses' mutilated bodies, and suffered psychological damage (Post Traumatic Stress Disorder) as a result. She brought an action against Railtrack PLC but the trial judge dismissed her claim, holding that she had failed to establish liability against Railtrack. She applied for permission to appeal.

The Court of Appeal granted permission to appeal, and suggested that the case was suitable for mediation. However, although the Claimant was willing, Railtrack PLC steadfastly refused to pursue that route.

When the matter came before the full Court of Appeal, the Court held (upon a technicality) that because the Claimant's appeal was based upon an issue that had not formed part of her original claim against Railtrack, her appeal consequently could not succeed. However, because of Railtrack's refusal even to consider mediation, the Court declined to grant Railtrack their costs, even though they had succeeded on appeal.

Lord Justice Henry Brooke, when delivering judgment in the case, referred to the autumn 2001 edition of the White Book Service 2001, and quoted the following passage:

The encouragement and facilitating of ADR by the court is an aspect of active case management which in turn is an aspect of achieving the overriding objective. The parties have a duty to help the court in furthering that objective and, therefore, they have a duty to consider seriously the possibility of ADR procedures being utilised for the purpose of resolving their claim or particular issues within it when encouraged by the court to do so. The discharge of the parties' duty in this respect may be relevant to the question of costs because, when exercising its discretion as to costs, the court must have regard to all the circumstances, including the conduct of all the parties (r.44.3(4), see r.44.5).

In the course of his discerning and perceptive judgment, Lord Justice Henry Brooke went on to state the following important words:

> ... when asked by the court why his clients were not willing to contemplate alternative dispute resolution, [Counsel] said that this would necessarily involve the payment of money, which his clients were not willing to contemplate, over and above what they had already offered. This appears to be a misunderstanding of the purpose of alternative dispute resolution. Skilled mediators are now able to achieve results satisfactory to both parties in many cases which are quite beyond the power of lawyers and courts to achieve. This court has knowledge of cases where intense feelings have arisen, for instance in relation to clinical negligence claims. But when the parties are brought together on neutral soil with a skilled mediator to help them resolve their differences, it may very well be that the mediator is able to achieve a result by which the parties shake hands at the end and feel that they have gone away having settled the dispute on terms with which they are happy to live. A mediator may be able to provide solutions which are beyond the powers of the court to provide. Occasions are known to the court in claims against the police, which can give rise to as much passion as a claim of this kind where a claimant's precious horses are killed on a railway line,

by which an apology from a very senior police officer is all that the claimant is really seeking and the money side of the matter falls away...

Lord Justice Brooke concluded in this way:

It is to be hoped that any publicity given to this part of the judgment of the court will draw the attention of lawyers to their duties to further the overriding objective in the way that is set out in Part 1 of the Rules and to the possibility that, if they turn down out of hand the chance of alternative dispute resolution when suggested by the court, as happened on this occasion, they may have to face uncomfortable costs consequences. In my judgment, in the particular circumstances of this case, given the refusal of the defendants to contemplate alternative dispute resolution at a stage before the costs of this appeal started to flow... the appropriate order on the appeal is no order as to costs.

The above cases were followed and endorsed in the case of *Hurst v Leeming* [2002] EWHC 1051 (Ch), when Mr Justice Lightman held that the following facts were *not* sufficient to justify a refusal to mediate, namely:

- that a party believed they had a 'watertight' case
- that a detailed refutation of the opposite party's case had already been supplied
- that an allegation of professional negligence had been made
- that heavy costs had already been incurred

The Judge in the *Hurst* case found that the only justification for refusing to participate in mediation, was that, on the facts of that case, mediation was not appropriate because it had no realistic prospect of success, only because of the character and attitude of one of the parties. The Judge went on to say that,

ordinarily a litigant would be taking a great risk by refusing mediation on this ground; but this was an exceptional decision and reflected how seriously disturbed the party's judgment was in relation to his case: *LTL 17/12/2001*

As a result of these cases, and no doubt several more by the date of publication, mediation has been given the important weight of judicial authority, and this backing by some of the most senior judges in the country has provided a significant boost to the mediation process, as well as imposing a very substantial risk in costs and judicial condemnation upon those who choose to ignore it.

Selecting a mediator

Once parties in dispute have sensibly agreed to mediate, their first task will be to find a suitable mediator. Little information is available to the public or to lawyers to assist them in this task. At present, there is no official overarching body incorporated to govern, regulate or represent mediators. There is no 'National Association of Mediators' and no government-approved institution to which the parties can turn. Regional associations of mediators have begun to emerge, as well as a growing number of companies set up specifically to market mediators and to provide mediation services, as for example, InterMediation Ltd in London. The most usual method presently used is to approach a mediator training institution, such as the School of Psychotherapy and Counselling at Regent's College, London, or CEDR (Centre for Effective Dispute Resolution). Some of these institutions may hold sufficient details of their accredited mediators to be in a position to recommend a suitable mediator, whether from their database, or by more personal knowledge or recollection. The Legal Services Commission Manual (April 2001, section 7) specifies five institutions (CEDR, ADR Group, Mediation UK, The Academy of Experts and the School of Psychotherapy and Counselling at Regent's College) whose trained and accredited mediators 'will for the time being be regarded as suitably qualified and capable of being funded under [Legal Aid] certificates'.

The Judicial Studies Board has a list of Mediation Service Providers, and this list is circulated to Judges and Courts throughout the United Kingdom. It is presumed that the list would be made available to parties who apply to the courts for assistance with the selection of a mediator. The Consumers Association and Citizens Advice Bureaux also have lists of mediation service providers.

Expert mediator or mediator expert

It is occasionally stated that for a successful mediation, the parties must feel that the mediator is a specialist in the *substance* of the dispute. This may accurately reflect the attitude of parties embarking upon mediation, and it highlights the ongoing debate as to whether a mediator should be an expert in mediation skills or an expert in the subject matter of the dispute. Although the answer will depend upon whether one is considering purely *facilitative* mediation or the more *evaluative* style, the thrust of the message taught in the mediator training at the School of Psychotherapy and Counselling at Regent's College is that it is more important for the mediator to be an expert in the skills than in the substantive field of the conflict.

The belief that it is essential for the mediator to be knowledgeable about the subject matter is often based upon a misconception, both as to the mediation process and the mediator's function. The principal misconception is that the mediator will decide the rights and wrongs of the respective cases of the parties, and that the mediator's role is to *impose* a solution or decision. It is understandable that with these images of the mediator's role being likened to that of a judge, the parties will expect an element of specialist knowledge or expertise. But in adopting such an approach the parties misconstrue the proper function of a mediator, who is neither a judge nor an arbitrator, but a 'facilitator', enabling parties to reach a settlement that makes sense to both of them.

There is a considerable body of opinion among writers on mediation to the effect that it is not necessary to select a mediator specializing in the area of dispute: see for example Professor Lawrence Susskind, 'Environmental Mediation and the Accountability Problem' (1981); Lela Love 'Top Ten Reasons Why a Mediator Should Not Evaluate' (1997); K. Mackie and Miles Marsh, *Commercial Dispute Resolution* (1995). The School's teaching is that selecting a substantive expert as a mediator involves a number of negative aspects. Every dispute is or tends to be sector-based and, with an expert who is also sector-based, a fresh approach to the dispute is more unlikely. A 'specialist' mediator may tend instinctively but inevitably to evaluate the strengths and weaknesses of each party's case. The parties will have reasonable expectations of impartiality, and evaluation by the mediator is the antithesis of impartiality.

On the other hand, there are those who firmly believe that a mediator without 'content knowledge' cannot be effective. They state that a mediator in a labour/management dispute, for example, who knows nothing of budgets, work schedules, personnel practices, regulatory or legal guidelines, precedents involving legal interpretation of contractual clauses, is not only ineffectual, but can be a stumbling block to an agreement: see Joseph B. Stulberg 'The Theory and Practice of Mediation: An Answer to Susskind' (1981). It can also be said that a mediator familiar with the area of the dispute is likely to be in a better position to raise alternative options for settlement, for he or she will be more familiar with the choices available than one who is outside that sector.

It is understandable that parties may feel more comfortable if the mediator is knowledgeable in the technicalities of their industry and, in some esoteric or highly technical disputes, it may be quite impossible for someone outside to act as an effective mediator. However, an expert in the field by no means guarantees greater prospects of settlement – in many instances rather the reverse. The mediator without specialist expertise will seek to obtain this knowledge from the parties themselves during the course of the mediation. This seldom causes irritation or impatience, but rather enables the parties to 'spout forth' about their particular field – often their pet subject – and creates a useful opportunity for the mediator to build rapport.

Code of conduct and insurance

There is, at present, no uniform Code of Conduct or Code of Ethics to which all mediators are bound. Generally, mediators will be bound by the codes of conduct or code of ethics produced by their own professions, or by the code of conduct of their Mediation Service Provider. (*See* for example CEDR's, The Law Society's or the ADR Group's Code of Conduct, or the Code of Practice of the British Academy of Experts.) Thus for example, barristers will be governed by the Bar's Code of Conduct, solicitors by the Law Society's code, psychotherapists by their College's code, and so on.

Parties should ensure that the mediator selected is adequately covered by professional indemnity insurance. The requirement for adequate insurance cover is frequently a requirement stipulated in the code of conduct, as for example in the Law Society's Code of Practice. The legal profession will normally be covered by their own professional indemnity insurers, mediation having been categorized as professional business. Insurance may be important, as it is not inconceivable that a mediator could cause financial loss by some error or misjudgment. The most common example would be where a mediator were accidentally or mistakenly to disclose to one of the parties a matter of extreme confidentiality and sensitivity, resulting in loss or damage to the other party. The 'injured' party might not unnaturally wish to seek recompense.

The pre-mediation agreement

Mediation is a consensual, informal and non-legal process. It has no rigid rules of procedure or evidence, and the parties will have agreed to enter into the process voluntarily. The solution or settlement is entirely in the parties' hands, with free options of setting their own standards for an acceptable outcome. Nevertheless, it is usually vital for the parties to enter into some form of pre-mediation agreement whereby the ground rules are clearly established. This will serve to protect all parties, including the mediator, from potentially difficult issues that can arise during the course of the mediation, and can help to obviate problems at a later stage in the mediation. Some of the issues that need to be addressed in the Mediation Agreement are set out below.

The role of the mediator

The parties may wish to stipulate in the Mediation Agreement that the mediator will be an impartial neutral who has no authority to impose a solution. However, they might also wish to leave open to themselves the option of varying the mediation to another form of ADR such as Early Neutral Evaluation, or Expert Determination. For example, if during the mediation the parties discover that the mediator is in fact an expert in the precise area of conflict involved and thus well placed to provide an authoritative opinion, they might consider inviting the mediator to determine the issue or the entire dispute one way or another. If the Mediation Agreement covered this eventuality, it would avoid arguments where one party wishes this to happen and the other party objects.

The conduct of the mediator

Ethical issues governing the conduct of the mediator need also to be addressed in the pre-mediation agreement. What is the mediator to do if one party reveals matters of a criminal nature, in confidence in the private caucus session? What is to happen if the mediator discovers matters which are likely to cause physical harm to another? Take for example a situation in a building dispute, where the architect reveals to the mediator that he has concerns about the design of the building, fearing that certain elements of the structure may be in danger of collapse. To disclose this information to the other side would clearly be a breach of the confidentiality which is so vital to the mediation process, yet to say nothing might endanger lives. Such circumstances should be addressed and catered for in the mediation agreement, and a clause similar to the following might be appropriate:

> Where any information is given or received which relates or gives rise to a material risk of harm, injury or other risk to safety, the duty of confidentiality shall not apply, save that the Mediator shall seek prior agreement from the parties as to the manner and extent of any disclosure to be made.

The Proceeds of Crime Act 2002 will also need urgent consideration. At the date of writing, the Law Society is in discussion with the government as to the effect of this statute upon mediation and mediators. Part 7 of the Act deals with money laundering and section 328 covers any person 'who enters into or becomes concerned in an arrangement which he knows or suspects facilitates the acquisition retention use or control of criminal property'. That section makes it a requirement to report or disclose ('make an authorised disclosure under section 338') any such activity to an authorized officer. However, section 333 also creates an offence of 'Tipping Off', whereby a person commits an offence if he 'makes a disclosure which is likely to prejudice an investigation'.

This puts any mediator in an invidious position. He is under an obligation of confidentiality to the parties, yet has a duty to disclose any suspicions. Furthermore he has a duty to stop the mediation in such circumstances, but will be unable to inform the parties as to the reason, for fear of contravening the 'tipping off' regulation. It therefore may be prudent for the mediator to cover this in the pre-mediation agreement and to lay the ground and prepare for the eventuality that the mediation may need to be terminated – without any reasons being furnished.

The liability of the mediator

It would be prudent to include in the Mediation Agreement a clause establishing the extent, if any, to which the mediator would be liable to any party for any act or omission in connection with the conduct of the mediation, including wilful misconduct.

The parties may also need to address the issue as to whether the mediator may be called as a witness or as an expert in any pending or subsequent litigation relating to the dispute or the subject matter of the mediation. They may wish to stipulate that the mediator may do so only where all parties agree in writing.

Attendance and representation at the mediation

A great deal of frustration, annoyance and embarrassment can be avoided by stipulating in the agreement precisely who will attend the mediation. The parties may wish to come alone or with their solicitor; they may want Counsel there as well; they may wish to have just their sales director present or their entire sales staff; they might want to bring a relative or friend. The decision as to who to 'bring along' may depend on 'what the other side are proposing to do', on the size of the venue or the wishes of the mediator. So concentrating the mind on these issues prior to the mediation itself and in the pre-mediation agreement serves a useful purpose. One advantage of the informality of mediation is that it allows much greater flexibility in the question as to who may attend. But there can be nothing more frustrating for a mediator than to commence the mediation with one party outraged or dismayed at the outset by the identity or number of persons attending on behalf of the other party.

Multi-party disputes also need especially careful consideration in terms of attendance and representation. Settlements may often depend upon all relevant parties being present and taking an active and positive part in the process. The absence of one or other crucial party may create a blockage to settlement.

Authority to settle

An issue that will benefit from being addressed in the pre-mediation agreement is that of ensuring that those attending the mediation have the necessary authority to reach a final binding agreement. The entire settlement can be frustrated by one party's lack of authority to settle without further instructions whether from insurer, solicitor, husband or chairman of the board.

The venue

The venue is usually also specified in the pre-mediation agreement. Careful thought should go into the choice of venue: it should ideally be at premises which incorporate separate rooms for each of the parties, sufficiently large to hold whatever entourage they have decided to bring, as well as a room for the mediator or mediators. The parties will need to feel sufficiently 'safe' and comfortable in their allotted rooms to be able to talk confidentially and in private. A safe and secure environment is one of the most essential requisites for a successful mediation. In the majority of mediations, one of the parties' solicitors will offer to make a suite of their offices available.

The parties and/or the mediator should also ensure that the venue is available for the full time allotted for the mediation. There is nothing more frustrating than to be close to settlement, and for a member of staff to come in and say: 'Sorry, I've got to lock up now.'

Confidentiality

It may be sensible to confirm in the pre-mediation agreement that the entire mediation process is confidential and will be conducted upon a 'without prejudice' basis. The parties may wish to stipulate, however, that any evidence that would otherwise be admissible or disclosable should not be rendered inadmissible or non-disclosable by reason only of its use in the mediation. The parties may also wish to address the question as to what should happen at the conclusion of the mediation to any written materials or documentation furnished to the mediator or to any party, and whether or not they should be returned without the mediator or the parties retaining copies.

An important issue related to confidentiality is whether or not there should be any stenographic, audio or visual record made or kept of the mediation process. Again, an express clause governing this in the agreement can avoid embarrassment, and ensure that all parties are clear as to this issue *before* they arrive at the mediation.

Duration of the mediation

The parties may wish or need to stipulate a finite time for the termination of the session or sessions. Alternatively, they may prefer to agree that the mediation will continue until the parties and the mediator are in agreement that the mediation has been unsuccessful; or until the mediator is of the view that further steps in the mediation process are unlikely to achieve a settlement; or until one party wishes to withdraw from the mediation. A clear understanding on the part of all parties as to precisely how long the mediation will last can save controversy. There are differing views as to whether the stipulation and strict adherence to a finite timetable is conducive to settlement. Some believe that if all parties are aware that at, say, 6 pm the mediation will terminate, with or without settlement, it serves to concentrate the mind and precipitate agreement. For as the deadline approaches, the parties are more likely to make concessions, in their desire not to leave without a settlement. Others consider that such strictures are not conducive to settlement, and prefer an open-ended stipulation as to duration. Many mediators with experience of the Court Pilot Mediation Schemes, where mediations are conducted strictly between 4.30 pm and 7.30 pm, will argue that the poor settlement rates encountered there are due to these difficulties of time.

The costs of the mediation

It is usual for the costs of the mediation to be shared equally between the parties, and a clause to this effect will normally be

included in the Mediation Agreement. An average fee for a mediator or a mediation is impossible to specify: fees for the mediator
can range from about £250 per day to £5000 or more per day,
depending upon a number of factors:

- the size or value of the dispute
- the length of time estimated or allowed for the mediation
- the amount of reading the mediator is expected to do prior to
  the mediation
- the importance of the settlement to the parties
- the additional services provided by the mediator (such as
  making available the venue or providing administrative assistance)

Pre-mediation preparation

Each party will need to submit to the mediator a case summary
setting out the nature of the dispute, together with such docu-
ments as they believe it is necessary for the mediator to read. The
amount of paperwork sent to the mediator may depend upon a
number of factors: the extent and size of the dispute, the length of
time that the matter has been in existence and the amount of detail
that the parties wish to disclose at the outset. The mediator will
also have a say in the matter. Some mediators prefer to have as little
information as possible: this allows them to acquire and discover
the necessary details concerning the issues directly from the parties during the mediation process; it also avoids the temptation to
pre-judge the issues or inadvertently to develop their own agenda
in the pre-mediation period. Others prefer as full a picture as
possible so as to fully appreciate the entire extent of the issues and
the underlying strategies.

What should be avoided in any event is for the parties to treat
the mediator as an arbitrator or judge, who needs to be persuaded
'on paper' of the respective strengths and weaknesses of each
party's case. It is not unknown for parties' legal representatives to
bombard the mediator with every item of evidence available in an

attempt to sway the mediator into 'recognizing the moral high ground' of their case. The mediator will have the opportunity of contact with the parties in the pre-mediation stage, provided he or she ensures that there is no appearance of partiality, and should encourage the submission of papers which disclose and concentrate upon their needs, interests and concerns.

Pre-mediation contact between the parties can be both helpful and productive. Issues can be clarified; they can be 'prioritized' so that the mediator acquires an insight into the relative importance or contentious nature of the various issues. This can assist the mediator in planning an appropriate strategy for the conduct of the mediation. For example, an effective strategy sometimes adopted by mediators is to deal with the less contentious issues first, and hopefully by achieving a 'settlement' on these issues, a momentum of movement towards accord is created in relation to further settlement on the more contentious or difficult issues.

> As the parties tentatively resolve the less controverted issues, they become psychologically committed to an overall settlement. Their focus on the mutually agreeable terms begins to convince them that the conflicted terms are not as important as they initially thought. They do not want to permit their substantial progress on the co-operative issues to be negated through impasses on the few remaining terms. As a result both sides become more amenable to settlement, making the mediator's job easier. (Brunet and Craver 1997)

Part III

Mock Mediation: Case Studies

Introduction to the Case Studies

In this section, a number of mock mediation Case Studies used on the Mediation Course at the School of Psychotherapy and Counselling (SPC) at Regent's College are analysed. The scenarios for the Case Studies are taken from classic legal cases which will be familiar to all lawyers.

The analysis is essentially conducted from two perspectives: firstly the case studies are considered from a psychological viewpoint, demonstrating how the parties and the mediator interact in the mediation in the light of the psychological aspects of conflict described in earlier chapters; secondly, the case studies are examined from a practical and procedural perspective, illustrating the methods and approaches adopted by the students at various stages in the SPC course. This analysis highlights some of the pitfalls and hazards that they – and many mediators – can encounter.

The diagrammatic wheels

Each Case Study's psychological analysis commences with a diagrammatic 'wheel'. These wheels are graphic representations intended to explain visually the characteristics of some of the givens that the mediator is likely to meet in mediation.

The sole function of the wheel is as a tool or a guide for gaining further psychological insight into mediation as a process, and is not to be used as a 'technique' by the mediator. Some will find the wheels of assistance as a guideline in understanding the paradigm, whereas others may prefer the textual explanations.

The circular format of the wheel outlines the psychological structure of the mediation process: the outer perimeter contains some of the unchangeable givens, the givens which we cannot alter; and the inner segments contain some of those givens that are characteristic to all of us, but in respect of which we have the power to create, invent and re-invent our approach, and to choose the way in which we engage, meet or deal with those givens.

The givens represented in the wheels are always interconnected *and yet* remain interdependent. The interconnections are not intended to be either chronological or linear representations of the mediation process, but rather to illustrate how an individual can respond to or engage with the givens. Thus the 'moving SELF', which always appears at the centre of all the wheels, in fact 'moves' through and 'shifts between' the various segments of the change-able givens. The contents of the various wheels thus overlap, and no individual wheel should be seen as a singular entity.

By storing this wheel at the back of the mind, the mediator may be able more readily to grasp the nature of some of the issues that the parties raise and, perhaps more importantly, those that they do not raise. Similarly, the wheel may help mediators 'bracket' their own prejudices and biases when mediating, and take a step backwards from the situation so that they can understand the experiences of the parties in a broader way. The wheels may also serve as a reminder to the mediator of the fundamentally interconnected nature of human existence: that each issue raised by the parties is connected to and should be seen in the context of others. Finally, they may also help mediators become aware of the importance of their own stance towards conflict.

8

Case Study 1

The Case of the Snail in the Ginger Beer
Donna Hew v Steve & Son

The facts

It was a hot summer evening in Paisley. Donna Hew, aged 44, visited a café and purchased a bottle of ginger beer. The café owner served the drink, pouring some of the ginger beer into a tumbler. When Donna Hew had finished her tumbler, she poured the remainder of the ginger beer into the tumbler. As she did so, a partly decomposed snail floated out of the bottle. The nauseating sight of the snail in her drink caused Donna Hew to suffer acute shock. Later, as a result of the impurities in the ginger beer she had already consumed, Donna Hew was struck down with severe gastroenteritis.

The case for Donna Hew

Donna Hew wishes to bring a legal action in respect of her injuries and losses. Her solicitors, Meek Wimpish & Softly have advised that no action can be brought against the café owner because the bottle arrived at the café properly sealed, and was made of dark opaque glass preventing any inspection.

Donna Hew's solicitors have discovered that Steve & Son, in the course of manufacture of the ginger beer, kept the bottles stored empty and uncovered in a cellar prior to being filled. However, the solicitors have advised Donna Hew that as the law stands at present she is unlikely to succeed in an action against Steve & Son because there is no contractual relationship between her and the manufacturers; and the snail cannot be regarded as a 'dangerous substance'.

Donna Hew has also been advised by her solicitors of the 'floodgates principle': that the courts are unlikely to extend the law to cover such matters for fear that this would 'open the floodgates' to many other actions. Indeed, her solicitor Mr Wimpish quoted the following passage from the judgment of Lord Anderson in a very similar case only 3 years previously:

> In a case where the goods of the Defendants are widely dis-tributed throughout Scotland, it would seem little short of outrageous to make them responsible to members of the public for the conditions of the contents of every bottle issuing from their works. It is obvious that if such responsibility attached to the Defendants, they might be called upon to meet claims which they could not possibly investigate or answer.

Ms Donna Hew is outraged. She cannot believe that Steve & Son can get away with such negligence. She is insistent upon pursuing the matter in court, having suffered losses and damage estimated to be in the region of £14,000, but has been persuaded, under the rules of court, to try mediation first. Privately, she has indicated to her solicitors that she would be prepared to accept a lesser sum in return for an apology and an admission of liability.

The case for Steve & Son

Mr Steve is furious. He has told his son 'dozens of times' to clean out the cellar, and now the reputation of this long-standing family firm is in grave jeopardy. He has some sympathy for Donna Hew, and feels morally obliged to her. But his solicitors have advised him that she has little or no case in law, and that the courts are unlikely to wish to extend the principles of liability. Yet he remains concerned that the publicity or a judgment against the firm, especially with these facts, would be disastrous for future sales. He has told his solicitors he would be prepared to pay up to £8000 but there must be no hint of an admission of liability, and there must be a confidentiality clause in any agreement.

Psychological Commentary

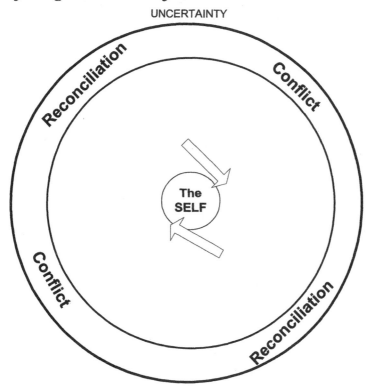

Figure 2 Aspects of conflict. The diagram represents a non-chronological and non-linear interconnection of some of the existential givens.

In this psychological commentary, the Case Study is considered from the perspective of the following aspects which are set out in the above diagrammatical wheel and which may affect the parties:

- uncertainty
- time and transiency
- the self: self-esteem and self-worth

The purpose of this wheel is to represent graphically 'conflict and resolution' as an ever-revolving cycle. It is an inevitable aspect of a cyclical dynamic that is in itself an inherent quality and part of natural human existence. Conflict is a given of the world and is always connected with self-esteem (see further below), and all other 'universally shared givens'.

Uncertainty

Uncertainty and inconsistency characterize every person's existence throughout his or her life from the very first day to the very last. The awareness of the inconsistency and the unpredictability of each moment of living lurks uncomfortably in the background of nearly every human activity. Uncertainty and the transient nature of human beings are universal unchangeable human givens or conditions.

These conditions are very prevalent in the mediation process and therefore need to be attended to by the mediator. Every individual responds to these givens in his or her own idiosyncratic manner; each person will experience this uncertainty in his or her own particular way. This is the uniqueness of existence.

In mediation, particularly in the caucus session, the mediator needs to deal with the anxiety and the apprehension which these 'givens' can invariably elicit. While seeking to establish a safe and trusting environment, the mediator must nevertheless provide both Donna and Steve with firm boundaries upon which they can rely with consistency and predictability. While total safety is impossible to create, the mediator needs to find the best methods of attaining as close to total safety as possible.

Both Donna and Steve will be subject to a number of anxieties and apprehensions created by the uncertainties of their position:

The dispute Donna cannot accept the legal advice that she has no case in law, yet to go against this advice has uncertain consequences. Steve is reassured by the legal position, but is uncertain as to the effect that other factors, such as adverse publicity, might have upon his business and the family reputation.

The mediation process Donna and Steve may have never previously taken part in a mediation: they will not know what to expect. Their lack of knowledge of the process can create its own uncertainty and this in turn will result in unease and trepidation.

The mediator Even if Donna or Steve have some experience of mediation, they will be concerned as to the quality and nature of the mediator: will the mediator be pleasant to deal with? Might the mediator immediately take sides with either Donna or Steve? Will the mediator be sufficiently effective to resolve the conflict?

The outcome In mediation, as in litigation, there is only one thing that is certain, and that is that the outcome is uncertain. Both Donna and Steve will be labouring under the heavy burden of uncertainty as to the outcome of the mediation.

Both Donna and Steve would clearly appreciate the comfort of certainty – the certainty of knowing how all the above questions will be answered. But that is not possible. It is another of the ambiguities and paradoxes that face both parties.

Time and transiency
Time and the impermanent nature of life are also reflected in the mediation sessions. Both Donna and Steve, as well as the mediator, will be subject to the effect of time, the impermanence of

each action and the transient nature of the mediation sessions. Here there is universality and inevitability, in that all of them will tend to respond to these uncertainties with feelings of insecurity: Donna, Steve and the mediator will each react in his or her own individual way.

Time limitation provides both a positive and a negative attribute to mediation. The positive side is the intensive nature of the encounter. Both Donna and Steve are aware that by the end of the mediation day, they will know whether or not there is resolution to their dispute and, if so, the nature and terms of that resolution. The negative aspect is the tendency for the mediation to be taken over by Donna's and Steve's – and the mediator's – desire for a quick resolution. This in itself can impede the process. Mediators can develop an overly strong desire to find a quick magic solution, with the result that, paradoxically, they themselves become counter-productive. The mediator needs to be permanently vigilant against this type of phenomenon and needs to suspend or put aside such feelings.

The Self

The desire for permanent protection of one's self-esteem is invariably a central issue in most conflict situations, hence it is an axiomatic ingredient in the mediation process. The common perception of 'self-esteem' is that of a static, stable mode of being; that low self-esteem is a negative state of mind, a feeling of inferiority, a 'disease' that needs to be 'cured' or eradicated; whereas high self-esteem is a state towards which people aspire and is a state to be maintained.

The term 'self-esteem' is defined in Webster's *Third New International Dictionary* (1981) as 'confidence and satisfaction in oneself'. According to this definition, the norm for human existence is assumed to consist of a state of *high* self-esteem and *high* self-worth. The word 'self-esteem' is therefore in itself ambiguous, for it may sometimes signify a high and sometimes a low state, depending upon the context of the situation.

It is from the assumption that self-esteem represents a positive attribute that the concept of 'positive thinking' or the 'win-win' philosophy of life is derived. Although this attitude serves a purpose on some occasions, it nevertheless has limitations and can produce devastating results, for example for one or other of the parties in the mediation. Imagine the situation where Steve approaches the mediation process with a positive attitude, firmly believing he will triumph over Donna. If he is unable to reach the settlement he expected, in spite of all his efforts, he may perceive the loss as a much greater setback to his self-esteem than had he come with a less positive attitude or lower expectations.

Alfred Adler's core theory about the inferior and the superior self has been referred to in Chapter 1. It may be worthwhile to return briefly to his philosophy. According to Adler, the conflict between inferiority and superiority is a basic human characteristic. Conflict stems from the human drive to become superior:

> to be a human being means the possession of a feeling of inferiority that is constantly pressing on towards his own conquest. (Adler, in Ansbacher and Ansbacher 1964)

There are many ways to visualize the 'self'. Some conceive of it as an unchangeable core self, or alternatively as a self that is constantly changing according to any particular meaning in life. The self or self-esteem fluctuates depending on the situation in which people find themselves. When their aspirations are frustrated, their self-esteem moves from a secure level to an insecure level, or from the insignificant to the significant (Spinelli 1989, Strasser 1999). The dynamic movement between low and high self-esteem is sometimes defined as a movement between a safe and an insecure self, or between a superior and an inferior self.

What people do to maintain their self-esteem depends partly upon their aspirations, their meanings and values, and their attitude to choices and change. In this Case Study, both Donna and Steve will adopt various strategies to protect their self-esteem. Donna may need money or monetary compensation to keep her self-image intact. Steve may need kudos, either for himself or his family business. He may need to maintain his superiority by aggressive behaviour; Donna may do the same by seeking to elicit respect, whether from Steve or from the mediator. The strategies for protecting their self-esteem will be as varied as they are individual people.

The mediator's assumption about self-esteem can also be of vital importance in mediation. If, for example, the mediator assumes that Donna's low self-esteem is a negative human trait and Steve's high self-esteem a positive one, then it might be difficult for the mediator to negotiate a 'good enough' settlement. It might be an impossible task for the mediator to seek permanently to maintain both Donna and Steve in a state of high self-esteem.

Conclusion

The mediator's awareness of and sensitivity towards the anxieties of Donna and of Steve, as precipitated by uncertainty, time and temporality, will greatly enhance the prospects of a safe and secure environment conducive to settlement. Furthermore, the mediator's recognition of the strategies that both Donna and Steve adopt to protect their self-esteem will place him or her in a much better position to move the mediation process on towards a satisfactory agreement.

In the final stages of this Case Study, as with most mediations, Donna and Steve are likely to embark upon a process of 'horse-trading' – strategic negotiation and positional bargaining. However, this will be of a wholly different nature to that described in Chapter 5 (Negotiate or Mediate?). Both Donna and Steve will have had a full and comprehensive opportunity to be truly heard. Their underlying motivations will have been revealed and their concerns and anxieties fully explored. They will have moved towards a working alliance.

Steve will thus make certain proposals for compensation and Donna will consider whether or not such proposals are adequate. Steve may or may not be prepared to raise the level of his offers if they are found unacceptable by Donna; and Donna may or may not lower her demands and expectations for settlement. Whether each of them does so, and to what extent, will largely be governed by the psychological aspects discussed above – Donna's and Steve's respective concerns as to uncertainty and time, and the degree to which either of them wish to maintain or protect their self-image and self-esteem.

The mediator who approaches these parties from a position of knowledge of the psychological aspects involved will be more effective in achieving a settlement.

Practical and Procedural Commentary

This Case Study is the first Case Study undertaken as a mock mediation on the School of Psychotherapy and Counselling's Mediation Course. It is conducted towards the end of the first session on the first day of the course, at a stage when very little mediation skills training has been given. The participants will have had a lecture and an exercise on 'Active Listening' but, apart from this and a brief overview of the mediation process, the participants will have had no other preparation for a 'trial run' at an actual mediation.

The Case Study is based upon a classic 'chestnut' legal case, *Donoghue v Stevenson* [1932] AC 562, which all law students learn about in their first year of law training. It is a simple case of a lady finding a decomposed snail in a ginger-beer bottle from which she had been drinking, and suffering physical and mental injury as a result. However, this 'simple' case went to the House of Lords and changed the entire course of legal jurisprudence. Prior to this case, an ultimate consumer was unable to sue a manufacturer in respect of a faulty product because of the absence of a contractual relationship between them. The House of Lords introduced the concept of a duty towards one's neighbour (the 'neighbour principle'), whereby the manufacturer's duty of care in negligence to the ultimate consumer was established.

With the advent of this momentous decision, the law of negligence was thrust into the twentieth century. (Christopher Walton, *Charlesworth & Percy On Negligence*, 10th edn, Chapters 14–48)

The papers given to participants for this first Case Study contain not only the facts for the mediator, but also the 'confidential brief' for both parties. Thus each participant, whether acting as mediator or role-playing a part, will be aware of the confidential brief for each side. In later mock mediations, the mediator receives the Case Study only, whereas the participants undertaking the role-plays receive the Case Study, as well as the Confidential Brief for the party whose role they are taking.

The mock mediation

The principal benefits of conducting the first mock mediation at a relatively early stage in the course are two-fold:

- the participants are presented with a graphic illustration of the difficulties and hazards that an untrained mediator is likely to encounter, and
- the participants acquire a dramatic benchmark for them to look back upon at the end of the course, to compare their performances 'then and now'

Many of the participants are lawyers who believe that, as they spend most of their time attempting to settle their cases, they will find mediation an entirely natural progression from their everyday skills and duties. Even non-lawyers and those who have chosen to come on the course because they feel it is something for which they have an aptitude or to which they will attune, believe that their daily encounters with conflict will have prepared them to mediate effectively. They are wrong.

From the outset, at the stage where the mediator opens the proceedings by introducing himself or herself to the parties, and introducing the parties to each other, the mediator can fall into an embarrassing trap: 'My name is John Smith. I would be happy if you called me John. May I call you by your Christian names?' This has already been referred to in Chapter 6 (What Actually Happens at a 'Legal' Mediation) and demonstrates how a simple *faux pas* can immediately create discomfort among the parties, and cause the mediator embarrassment.

The student mediator on the first mock mediation is often oblivious to the importance of the seating arrangements. Yet this is another aspect of comfort. Students on the course are repeatedly told that one of their prime functions as a mediator is to 'create a safe environment'. The safe environment is one that is conducive to openness and will lead most readily to a settlement in a 'meeting of minds and spirits'. Such an environment cannot be created if the parties are uncomfortable. Quite often the parties will be most apprehensive about being in the same room together, let alone sitting at the same table. So if the mediator arranges the seating so that the parties are virtually rubbing shoulders, he or she will have unwittingly created an atmosphere of tension or unease, which is wholly counter-productive to that 'safe environment' that an effective mediator will aspire to create.

Similarly, if the mediator gives little or no thought to the issue, he or she will have done the parties – and the process – little service. Thus an invitation to 'Please sit where you like ...' will simply place the parties in embarrassment: they will not know where to put themselves; they may instinctively wish to place themselves as far away as possible from the other party, but then discover that they are, as a result, sitting too far away from the mediator; they may even go for the same seat, as if they were in a final round of 'musical chairs'. Any shuffling and changing of chairs will only serve to create discomfort and embarrassment. The trainee mediator is therefore taught to give this aspect careful consideration, so as to enable the mediation at least to get off to a good start!

Opening statements

Once the mediator has given his or her opening address, he or she is taught to invite the parties to give their 'opening statements'. Here again the unskilled mediator can fall into a trap: 'Which one of you would like to give the first statement? Who would like to start? Which of you would like to speak first?'

These are some of the ways that the untrained mediator embarks upon the opening statements in this first Case Study. Participants are taught that they must set the boundaries of the mediation process in order to achieve a safe environment. But by asking the parties who would like to start, the mediator is to some extent abdicating from that responsibility. This again risks the creation of tension and unease, because:

- one party might prefer to start first, but is unwilling to say so
- one party may be upset if the other volunteers first
- both parties may be reluctant to go first
- both parties might simultaneously volunteer to start

The participant is thus taught to take a certain control of the process and to decide, possibly in advance, who he or she will ask to go first. This may avoid an embarrassed silence while the mediator looks from one to the other, waiting for a volunteer. The mediator should also consider the preparation of a short explanation as to the reason for making the choice of who goes first so as not to cause offence, upset or suspicion.

First private caucus session

Experienced lawyers and other mature professionals – some who, as stated above, think of themselves as natural born mediators – find that they are at a total loss for words or questions when they come to do their first mock mediation. The participants undertaking the *Donna Hew* mediation are frequently at a loss to know how to proceed. They are perplexed, confused and unable to act.

FACT-FINDING
They therefore resort to fact-finding. This is a process with which

most lawyers are familiar and comfortable; they do this whenever taking instructions from clients. Non-lawyers find it equally secure to ask fact-finding questions because it is a natural process for any reasonably and normally inquisitive individual. Thus the following type of exchange tends to take place:

MEDIATOR	So what time was it when you went into this café for your ginger beer?
DONNA	About 4.00 pm.
MEDIATOR	And have you done this regularly?
DONNA	No. Occasionally.
MEDIATOR	Have you been frequenting this café for a long time?
DONNA	About a couple of years.
MEDIATOR	Has anything like this happened before?
DONNA	No.
MEDIATOR	Did you complain immediately?
DONNA	Yes, of course.
MEDIATOR	And what did they say?
DONNA	They just offered me another bottle.

This may or may not all be interesting, but where has it taken the mediator? The trainee mediator soon runs out of fact-finding questions and 'dries up' completely. The series of closed questions has achieved very little in terms of discovering the real or underlying aspects of the dispute, if any, and has done nothing to move the party towards a common ground from which a settlement might evolve.

A trained mediator might have adopted the following line of questioning, which some might say would be more effective:

Could you share with me your feelings about Steve & Son's opening statement?
Can you tell me how this whole matter has affected you?
How do you see Steve & Son's position?
Would you like to give me your thoughts on their proposals?
How did you feel about their reaction to your claim?

I hear from your opening that there is a certain amount of anger. Could you perhaps explain a little more what it is that makes you angry in this case?

If the above line of questions precipitate answers which contain a greater wealth of information, then they might be followed up with a series of prompts which could secure even further disclosures, for example:

Can I explore a little further...
Could you tell me a little more about...
Can I clarify...
Would you like to share with me...
Can you help me a little more with...

Questions along these lines may be more effective in encouraging Donna to open up and to give an account of her side of the story in the fullest possible manner. The intention is to 'push a series of buttons that will open the floodgates' and allow Donna to speak freely and candidly. In this way, the mediator will obtain the greatest amount of *material* information which he or she can then use to find that common ground.

GETTING TO THE 'BOTTOM LINE'

Another extremely common phenomenon that emerges in the *Donna Hew* Case Study is this: when participants approach their first mock mediation, relatively untrained and inexperienced, there is invariably a strong desire to get straight to the 'bottom line' of each party's bargaining position. This frequently occurs at the outset of the first caucus and the question presents itself in a variety of forms. Some participants express it directly: 'What is your bottom line?' Others vocalize the enquiry in a number of different ways:

What would you be prepared to accept?
What would you suggest is a reasonable settlement for you?

Have you thought about the minimum level of payment that
you would accept?

Are you looking for a specific figure in terms of a monetary
compensation?

Do you have a bottom-line figure in mind?

What would you expect or like to see coming from the other
side in terms of payment?

What is the least that you would be happy walking away with?

Tell me what you consider to be your absolute goal?

The practice of asking a party to specify their 'bottom line' is
fraught with dangers and bristling with difficulties.

- Money may not be the prime objective
  Firstly, the question assumes that money is the party's prime
  objective – and invariably it is not. On frequent occasions, a
  mediator will find that 'money' is merely a vehicle for the party's emotions. As stated earlier, all disputes involve injury to
  feeling, and one party may be experiencing immeasurable anger and hurt with the other side about the way they have been
  treated. When this occurs their prime objective is to hurt, damage and wound the other side as severely as possible – and
  their perception is invariably that the most effective way of
  achieving such damage is 'to hit them where it hurts the most
  – in their pocket!'

- Parties unsure of their bottom line
  Secondly, the parties to the dispute often do not know what
  their bottom line is when they embark upon mediation. They
  may not yet have fully thought it through at such an early stage;
  or it may depend upon a number of other factors, such as
  whether the money is accompanied by an apology or an acknowledgment, or whether some other tangible benefit can
  be extracted from the settlement.

- Parties may not tell the truth
  Thirdly, if asked for their bottom line and assuming they have

considered the issue and have an answer, the party may not tell the mediator the truth. At an early stage in the process the parties have often not yet been able to verify their trust in the mediator, and may not be sure as to his or her approach to negotiations. Invariably they see the mediator as a negotiator on their behalf and the old instincts as to positional bargaining come to the fore:

> If we tell the mediator that £50,000 is our bottom line we'll probably end up with £30,000. So let's tell him our bottom line is £70,000.

More important, perhaps, is the fact that the mediator will not know or cannot be sure whether the parties have told the truth. If he or she then proceeds upon the basis of what he or she has been told and takes it at face value, the issue may rebound upon the mediator at a later stage in the process.

- Parties put in a quandary as to what to say
Fourthly, by asking a party to specify their bottom line, the mediator is thereby 'putting them to their election' as to what to say:

> Do we tell the truth or not?

A sensitive mediator should not put the parties in such a position where they are placed in a dilemma as to what to reveal to the mediator. Such a position creates a rift between them and hinders the process of free and open exchange of information.

- Parties are 'fixed' with their bottom line
Fifthly, having once revealed to the mediator what they claim to be the lowest figure acceptable – or the highest figure they are prepared to pay – it becomes increasingly difficult for the parties to move from that position. They will fear 'losing face', or appearing weak, or not being seen as truthful in the eyes of the mediator, and may thus be tempted or inclined to hold out to their original position for longer than they might otherwise

have done. This severely limits the 'manoeuvrability' of the mediator in the task of getting the parties to shift from entrenched positions.

It is not necessarily the case that a mediator should *never* seek to ascertain the parties' 'bottom lines', but rather that it should be done in a more subtle and effective way, and not at a very early stage in the mediation process. It is entirely understandable that the mediator should be eager to establish the lowest or highest area of common ground between the parties: he or she will feel that it is the only way to determine whether a settlement is possible, as well as the only means by which they can start working towards that common ground. But trainee mediators should resist this temptation in the early phases of the mediation. They are taught to ascertain the parties' bottom line in a more general and less direct way. By discovering aspects of the parties' world-view, and their overall approach to settlement and to monetary compensation, the mediator will be better able to distil from that the true and genuine position as to the true optimum outcome for each party. In this way, the mediator will be in a good position to work with the parties towards achieving that objective.

The following are some tentative suggestions of possibly more effective ways to put questions which will provide the party's view of settlement:

What would a settlement here do for you?

How would a monetary settlement affect you and your family?

How do you see this dispute being settled?

Can you tell me about your thoughts for a good outcome to this dispute?

How would a compensation payment leave you?

Is there a way in which you think this matter might satisfactorily be resolved?

Conclusion

By the end of this first mock mediation the participants on the course are beginning to appreciate the very different qualities that they will be required to demonstrate as effective mediators. Many of the qualities are far removed from those that they have acquired instinctively as lawyers or as other professionals. They will have learnt that fact-finding and 'closed questions' are not effective or helpful in moving the mediation process forward, and merely stagnate their ability to get to the nub of the dispute. They will have noted that their usual abilities in dealing with people in their own daily lives need to be honed and advanced in a particular way if they are to mediate disputes successfully. Their instincts for being judgmental, for making assumptions and for attempting to secure a quick settlement all need to be resisted and discarded.

An entire world of new skills lies ahead.

9

Case Study 2

The Case of the Misleading Banker's Reference

Heavenly Burn v Hell, Err & Partners

The facts

Heavenly Burn are advertising agents. They were instructed by their clients, Caneasily Pay Ltd to secure substantial quantities of television time and newspaper space for a concerted advertising programme. This advertising was to be paid for initially by Heavenly Burn in their capacity as agents for and on behalf of Caneasily Pay, but following placement of the order Heavenly Burn would expect reimbursement from Caneasily Pay.

Wishing to confirm the financial position and status of Caneasily Pay, Heavenly Burn sought a 'Banker's Report' from Hell, Err & Partners, who were merchant bankers with whom Caneasily Pay had their principal account. A letter was sent to Hell, Err & Partners requesting their opinion

> in confidence as to the respectability and standing of Caneasily Pay and whether you consider them trustworthy in the way of business to the extent of £1m per annum of advertising contract.

Hell, Err & Partners replied:

For your private use and without responsibility on the part of this Bank. . . . Caneasily Pay is a respectably constituted company, considered good for its ordinary business engagements. Your figures are larger than we are accustomed to. Yours etc.

On the faith of this statement, Heavenly Burn placed advertisements totalling £170,000. Unfortunately, a short while later Caneasily Pay went into liquidation, for a relatively small sum, and were unable to reimburse Heavenly Burn for the advertising costs.

Heavenly Burn wish to bring an action against Hell, Err & Partners, for negligently providing the reference. They contend that the reference was given in a commercial context with banks being in a special position of knowledge of their client's financial situation. Knowing that the reference would be relied and acted upon, the Bank ought not to be permitted to shield behind the disclaimer. Hell, Err & Partners argue that as Bankers, they have a primary duty to their own customers and therefore use guarded references. They will say 'light grey' instead of 'black'. The information was given gratuitously and in confidence, with an express disclaimer of liability.

The parties have agreed to mediate their dispute. Mr Heavenly and Mr Hell will attend the mediation together with the Bank's solicitor.

Confidential brief: Mr Heavenly

Mr Heavenly was the prime mover in securing the contract with Caneasily Pay. He has been advised in relation to the dispute that banks have a special position in law in relation to the giving of references. Such references are a vital part of the business world and thus a bank has a special duty of care. Mr Heavenly has told his partners that, in seeking the Banker's Report, he had done all that a prudent businessman would have done. On a point of principle, therefore, the partners have agreed that a claim should be vigorously pursued at all costs.

Privately, however, Mr Heavenly accepts that he threw caution to the wind. He was overwhelmed by the size of the orders that Caneasily Pay wished to make, and the prospect of accumulating very considerable profits on the deal proved too great a temptation. He was aware that, on a previous occasion, a cheque from Caneasily Pay had to be re-presented before finally being paid. Thus he feels that he should perhaps have secured other guarantees, especially as the letter from the bank was not very explicit.

He has not told his partners about the previous 'bounced' cheque and very much hopes that this will not come out. He is therefore anxious that the mediation will provide a satisfactory solution.

Confidential brief: Hell, Err & Partners

Mr Hell, in the face of his partners, is adamant that the Bank should not be liable. He states that the Bank were only asked for their opinion and therefore did not place themselves in the position of financial advisers to Heavenly Burn. 'If you ask a policeman for the quickest route from A to B, that does not render him a traffic adviser liable to you if he is wrong.' The Bank has a prime duty to its own customer, hence the guarded terms of the reference. Furthermore the disclaimer could not have been more clear.

Privately, however, Mr Hell was aware of the fact that Caneasily Pay ran their overdraft constantly at its limit, and indeed were very substantially indebted to the Bank. Mr Hell felt that if he gave a good reference, the advertising might produce a significant upturn in the financial fortunes of Caneasily Pay, which in turn could alleviate their indebtedness to the Bank. For this reason he attempted to couch the reference in as favourable – but Delphic – terms as possible, reassured that there was an express disclaimer.

The Bank's reputation would be shattered if it became publicly known that the Bank had allowed its own position to influence the giving of a reference. Mr Hell's own position would also be untenable, and at his age this would be nothing short of catastrophic. However, his partners expect a good result from the mediation, having been told that right is on their side. Mr Hell therefore cannot be seen to return from the mediation process empty-handed.

Psychological Commentary

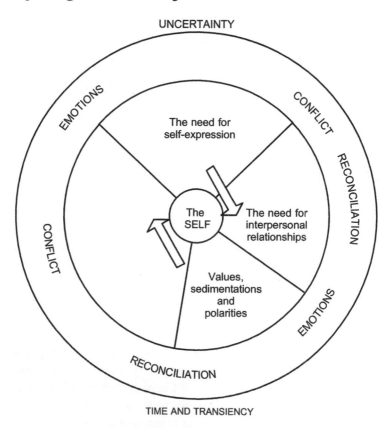

Figure 3 Aspects of conflict.
The diagram represents a non-chronological
and non-linear interconnection of some of the existential givens.

This wheel, as the previous wheel, depicts two of the unchangeable givens, Uncertainty and Temporality, surrounding the cycle of conflict and resolution, with emotions interspersed. Added to this now are some changeable givens, namely the need for self-expression, the need for interpersonal relationships, and the creation of values, sedimentations and polarities. This psychological commentary considers how in the above Case Study, Mr Heavenly and Mr Hell, as well as the mediator, might be affected by these psychological aspects of conflict.

The need for self-expression and interpersonal relationships
The need for self-expression and the need to create interpersonal relationships are closely interconnected. Both are natural, humanly shared characteristics. Interpersonal relationships are formed in response to the uncertainties and the temporality of the world. The moment people are born, they are thrown into this world with others and relate to each other. This is a prerequisite of living; they cannot escape relationships or avoid relating. Connected with this condition is the need for people to express themselves and, as seen in Chapter 3 (Communication Skills), parties have a fervent desire to be heard.

Both Mr Heavenly and Mr Hell are unlikely to be reticent if listened to appropriately by the mediator. They will both be eager to seek to persuade the mediator of the strength of their relative positions: Mr Heavenly, by requesting a Banker's reference, did all that a prudent businessman would be expected to do in his position; and Mr Hell will be equally adamant that the Bank, in providing the reference with a strong caveat, conducted itself entirely as it should.

By the careful and apposite use of silence, and by tuning-in and sensitively 'reflecting back' some of the significant elements of their narrative, the mediator can provide the space, the time and the trusting environment for both Mr Heavenly and Mr Hell to fulfil their inexorable human desire to express themselves freely. The less actively the mediator intervenes, the more likely he is to create conditions of calm in an empathic, trusting environment. Heavenly and Hell may thus feel freer to express their innermost concerns and thereby reveal their true anxieties in the dispute. Once they have started to tell their tale, they will inevitably reveal relevant parts of their world-view. This will provide the mediator with the opportunity to expose the hidden motivations that may eventually enable rapprochement and settlement to take place.

Mr Heavenly and Mr Hell, through their desire for self-expression, will seek to create a bond with the mediator. This may ostensibly be for the purpose of 'getting the mediator on their side', but in reality it may be little more than a means of facilitating their need for self-expression. The greater the bond, the more comfortable they will feel making certain disclosures.

The mediator has a clear and urgent purpose in 'relating' to both Mr Heavenly and Mr Hell. The rapport and trust that is required to enable free and candid disclosures must be established as quickly as possible. Through an appreciation of his or her own 'relatedness' with both Mr Heavenly and Mr Hell, and the knowledge that he or she shares many of the givens and limitations of the world, the mediator can put himself or herself in the shoes, first of Mr Heavenly in the caucus session with him and then, in turn, in the shoes of Mr Hell. This process can then create a more empathic relationship, a relationship more conducive to openness and candour.

Values, sedimented (rigid) values, polarities and aspirations (see also Figure 5, page 172)
We all create values. These spiritual, moral or behavioural codes provide 'meaning' and serve to create a variety of strategies for living. Such values and belief systems may sometimes become rigid and difficult to 'shift', and may then be referred to as 'sedimentations' – similar to matter that settles at the bottom of a liquid which may require vigorous stirring to move it. Sedimentations can frequently be positive; but when too rigid, they can be detrimental and problematical. Yet sedimentation can in

theory always be shifted (Spinelli 1989, and Strasser and Strasser 1997). An awareness of this human propensity is of paramount importance to mediators.

If the mediator is able to identify Mr Heavenly's or Mr Hell's value system, he or she will be in a position to recognize and understand their motivations both in the dispute and in the mediation. Indeed, if the mediator is able to uncover their world-view, he or she will discover that Heavenly and Hell share similar elements of their value system: *over-zealous ambition*. They both threw caution to the wind; they both risked their precious careers for the sake of improving their own position; they both conducted their business on the very edge of propriety – all to feed their own ambition and augment their self-esteem.

This shared element of their value system clearly provides an obvious basis of commonality between these adversaries. If Mr Heavenly is able to appreciate that Mr Hell's actions were moti-vated by precisely the same rationale and by similar underlying principles, his anger at the Bank will be dissipated. Once the anger, bitterness and sense of betrayal are removed, the parties will realize that they are both in the same predicament, from which they must both attempt to emerge unscathed. They have then moved from an adversarial stance to a working alliance.

POLARITIES

As soon as people create values, they create polarities. When something is good, it presupposes that something else must be bad. Polarities are important factors to consider in mediation. They can be positive or negative, depending upon the perspective or the context and the circumstances: for example, strength can in some circumstances be negative whereas weakness can equally be positive. Polarities may also complement each other and are not necessarily antagonistic.

With their shared values of powerful ambition, people such as Mr Heavenly and Mr Hell probably despise apathy. They probably cannot abide those who simply go about their day-to-day employment without any view to advancement of their careers.

Equally, they may view loyalty and disloyalty as polarities: loyalty to their company or Bank is to be commended and disloyalty condemned. Yet through their desire to be loyal and by virtue of their actions, they have both in fact been disloyal. They have brought the company and the Bank into disrepute.

Once again, if the mediator in the caucus sessions is able to unearth these factors, and use these ambiguities to challenge and confront the parties in an empathic way, he or she will be able more effortlessly to facilitate a settlement.

Practical and Procedural Commentary

Introduction

This Case Study, the second mock mediation exercise on the course, is conducted at the end of the second session on the first day of the course. By this stage, and since conducting the first mock mediation, the participants on the course will have had a lecture, together with an exercise, on 'Values and Value Systems'. They will also have had their second lecture and an exercise on Communication Skills, dealing with 'Reflecting Back', 'Paraphrasing', 'Summarizing', and 'Focusing'.

This Case Study is similarly based upon the classic legal authority of *Hedley Byrne & Co. Ltd v Heller & Partners Ltd* [1964] A.C. 465, again a case which all law students learn about in their first year of law training, in their Tort lectures. The case established the principle whereby a person who makes a negligent misstatement may owe a duty of care to another person who places reliance upon that statement and then suffers economic loss as a result: the maker of the statement could be liable for the loss suffered.

The Case Study contains similar 'hidden agendas' to those existing in reality in the true case of *Hedley Byrne v Heller & Partners*. The advertising company in that case, Easipower Ltd were truly heavily indebted to their merchant bank, Heller & Partners, and the Bank did indeed hope to benefit financially from the advertising campaign financed by Hedley Byrne. In fact, an allegation of fraud had originally been made by the then Plaintiffs, but was later withdrawn.

The Case Study enables the participant role-players to embellish the concept of the reputation of the parties, thereby demonstrating the importance of values and value systems.

The opening address

The participants by now have grasped the importance of the mediator's opening address and the need to make it authoritative, yet at the same time setting an appropriate tone for the 'safe environment' that is so imperative for a successful mediation.

Many participants allow themselves to be deflected by an excessive concern that they may get the opening address wrong. They have a fear of missing out an important element of the opening address. Others become embarrassed when they realize they have left something out or made a mistake. They may go through their opening statement with the feeling that there is one vital matter they need to state, but they 'cannot for the life of them remember it!'

All these phenomena could be alleviated by the use of an 'aide memoire' or 'crib sheet'. Some of the most experienced mediators have in front of them when they make their opening statement a set of notes itemizing each of the matters they must address: thus they will list some or all of the following: the mediator's role and the role of the various parties, the nature and purpose of mediation, the importance of confidentiality, the 'Without Prejudice' nature of the process, the need to check that the parties have authority to settle, the procedure to be adopted, the ground rules, timing and an explanation of the facilities available. In this way, the mediator can concentrate on the tone and manner of the opening, without becoming preoccupied with getting the content correct.

Following the parties' opening statements

The parties have given their opening statements. What does the mediator do next? Here again is an opportunity taken by many participants to allow themselves to be deflected from proper procedure.

Participants are sometimes tempted to invite the parties to respond to the other's opening statement:

Do you wish to reply to what has just been said?
Is there anything you would like to come back on?
You will have an opportunity to speak later, but is there anything else you would like to say now?
Do you want just to deal with that last point?
Have you said everything you want to say?

The danger of inviting responses is that this relatively short opening process can very easily descend into a 'shouting match' or get out of hand. If one party is allowed to respond, then the other will, not unnaturally, wish to do likewise. And the danger is that this can continue to the extent that the mediator may eventually be obliged to interrupt, similar to a referee stepping in between contestants. The mediator needs to bear in mind that at this early stage, the parties will still be very much in adversarial mode. They may remain wary or suspicious as to any step the other takes to 'win over' the mediator; they will be anxious to maintain equality and a 'level playing field'. Similarly the mediator will perhaps not yet have had sufficient time or opportunity to demonstrate his impartiality and to create trust in both parties equally.

Trainee mediators are often tempted to make a comment upon, or seek clarification of, one or other party's opening statement – with the possibility or danger that their comment can be misinterpreted: 'Is that all you want to say?' This innocent question can easily be interpreted as an early indication of partiality. Take for example, the following question: 'So you are not seeking the whole amount of the claim?' Again, by this simple question, possibly nothing other than a pure attempt at clarification, the mediator can unwittingly create an impression that he or she has formed a (judgmental) view of the merits of one party's case over the other.

Often the best advice is for the mediator simply to thank the parties and move swiftly on to the private caucus session.

The first caucus

Although many of the communication skills have been dealt with in the first two 'skills lectures', the participants remain in conditioned mode. The lawyers and non-lawyers alike continue to 'fact-find', to allow themselves to reveal their own views by some of their questions, to be judgmental and to be overly 'solution focused' – in other words, 'diving in' when the merest glimpse of a solution appears to present itself. Some examples may serve to illustrate, as follows:

JUDGMENTAL QUESTIONS

So taking this reference was a bit of a gamble on your part?

Have you not had experience of references in the past?

Do you think there were more checks you might have made?

Why did you not query the disclaimer?

Have you considered that your solicitors might be right when they were sceptical of your chances?

Wasn't it a little unreasonable to expect them to make further credit checks?

Such questions may simply 'slip out', because the mediator is human and has not yet learned, or is unable to 'bracket' his or her own feelings or views. Quite often a party will utter something that appears so extreme or unreasonable that there is an overwhelming temptation on the part of the mediator to say something like: 'Don't you think that is a little irrational?' Participants are taught that such slips of the tongue – if that is what they are – need not be entirely fatal and can usually be rectified. On the SPC course, students are encouraged to 'rewind' the tape and start again or simply to rephrase the question. In a true mediation, however, there may be nothing wrong in endeavouring to retrieve the situation by saying something along the following lines:

I'm sorry, that sounds very judgmental, let me rephrase that question.

Sorry, let me put that in another way.

I didn't mean it to sound quite like that, let me put it this way...

SOLUTION-FOCUSED QUESTIONS

In the early stages, the student mediator will have a number of preconceived notions of where the fault lies, who is more to blame and where the solution can be found. This often leads to 'cross-examination' type questions, designed to reveal a chink in the armour of one or other party:

Ah, so you accept that there was some fault on your side?

So it *was* a bit of a gamble?

So full reimbursement is not necessarily your prime objective?

You are prepared to compromise on that, are you?

These interventions on the part of the mediator serve only to say: 'I've caught you out now, I've spotted your weakness and I can work on that to persuade you to make concessions and to drive you to a settlement'. This is not likely to assist in creating rapport.

Participants are warned repeatedly against being preoccupied with finding a solution. They are told to shed from their own shoulders that burden of responsibility of reaching a settlement, and to remind themselves constantly that the responsibility for reaching a settlement lies fairly and squarely *with the parties*. The mediator can do only so much to facilitate accord but, if the parties are unwilling or unable to move from their entrenched positions, then the mediator must detach himself or herself from blame.

The participants are taught to *explore* solutions; to be alert to possibilities that the parties may not have thought of; to embrace the concept of lateral thinking or 'thinking out of the box' – but that they should not allow themselves to be or to become preoccupied with the thought that 'a solution is there for the taking – if only I could find it'.

ENDING THE CAUCUS

Timing of the caucus session is again a problem. In this second Case Study, the participants are still finding difficulties with questioning and this frequently leads to a complete neglect of the time factor.

THE 'HAND ON THE DOOR' SYNDROME

It is in this session that the Participants are taught about the curious phenomenon commonly referred to as the 'Hand on the Door' Syndrome. It occurs when the mediator is concluding the caucus session – possibly just leaving the room to move on to the next caucus with the other party, or showing one party to the door – when the party makes a statement such as: 'I think there is one thing that perhaps you should know about Caneasily Pay – they once bounced a cheque . . .'; or 'Can I just mention that the Bank were quite keen for the advertising to go ahead as it would have improved Caneasily Pay's credit balance . . .'. The caucus has just come to an end, and one party seems compelled to make some form of 'confession' – a gem of a disclosure or a wholly new issue is raised. What is the mediator to do? The caucus has probably already overrun its allotted time span and the other side may be getting impatient – if not fearful or suspicious. Yet to end the session there without exploring these matters further might seem counter-productive.

Participants are taught that in such circumstances, the wisest course of action is perhaps to stay with the party in caucus, and pursue the matters that have just been raised. The party clearly wishes to 'get something off their chest' and it is usually vital to take the opportunity to 'stay with it'. However, it is *vital* to let the other side know what is happening, and this can be done with considerable advantage by words of encouragement, such as: 'We are just on to a line of exploration that I feel could be very productive – so we may be a little longer on this session . . .'; or 'An issue has been raised which in my view could be very useful to explore further, bear with me for a little longer . . .'; or 'I am aware that we have been some time, but I think the time is being spent extremely productively, so a little patience may be well rewarded . . .'

CONFIDENTIALITY AND 'TAKING MATTERS ACROSS TO THE OTHER SIDE'

Finally, it is most important to conclude a caucus session with a reminder of the confidential nature of all the discussions that have just taken place. The sight of the mediator disappearing along the corridor to speak to the other side can frequently engender feelings of anxiety as to what will be discussed behind those closed doors. Anything the mediator can do to alleviate these fears will be beneficial to the process. An assurance that everything he or she has been told has been received in the strictest confidence and will not be revealed to the other party can usually allay most fears.

It is thus a constructive and an important part of the process to check whether there is anything that might *usefully* be imparted to the other side. Invariably the trainee mediator will realize that they neglected to obtain permission from one party to discuss certain matters with the other which might now prove helpful. Thus the failure or omission to ask: 'Is there anything that we have discussed just now that you think might assist the process if it were revealed to the other side?' can lead to a stultifying effect upon the mediator's approach in the second caucus. 'I wish I had checked whether I could raise this with them!'

Ascertaining whether and what, if anything, can be taken across to the other side is however a sensitive issue. The mediator should not ask permission to take something across as a matter of course, or at the end of each caucus session: for this would create an impression that there is an expectation on the part of the mediator that the party will furnish some material to take to the other side. But occasionally it is useful for the parties to provide the mediator with some material that might form the basis of exploration in the next caucus.

Conclusion

The end of the second Case Study leaves the participants with the clear understanding that mediation is not as easy as they once thought it would be. They begin to appreciate that the psychological aspects taught on the course can provide them with an invaluable added insight into the parties and the conflict as presented in front of them. But much lies ahead still to be learned and the students on the course approach the prospect with keen anticipation.

10

Case Study 3

The Case of the Collapsed Reservoir and the Flooded Colliery

Highlands v Stretcher

The facts

Scot Highlands is the owner of certain coal mines at a colliery known as the Red Face Colliery. The neighbouring land is owned by Lord Stretcher who recently constructed a large water reservoir upon his property.

During the course of excavation of the bed of the reservoir, Lord Stretcher's engineers had discovered 5 disused mine shafts going down vertically some 200 feet. These shafts had been filled with a mixture of rubble and clay. Unbeknown to the engineers, the foot of each shaft was connected by a horizontal passage to the vertical shafts of the mines at the neighbouring Red Face Colliery. Shortly after the reservoir was filled with water, the vertical shafts beneath the reservoir bed gave way and water flooded along the horizontal passages into the colliery, causing considerable damage. The colliery was closed for 4 weeks and 34 men were laid off during that time.

Scot Highlands claims as follows:

Cost of remedial works to mine shafts	£170,000
Loss of profits	£250,000
Lost wages (34 × £500 per week for 4 weeks)	£ 68,000
Total	£488,000

Lord Stretcher contends that the reservoir collapsed as a result of the horizontal passages beneath his land, constructed by the Colliery in previous years, and of which Scot Highlands ought to have had notice. He wishes to counterclaim:

Reconstruction costs	£340,000
Loss of water rate revenue	£ 48,000
Damages for the loss of his reputation, say	£100,000
Total	£488,000

The parties have agreed to mediation. Those attending: Lord/Lady Stretcher, and 'Big' Redface, the manager of the colliery on behalf of Scot Highlands.

Confidential brief: Mr Redface (on behalf of the Redface Colliery)

'Big' Redface, as he is affectionately known, is the manager of the Red Face Colliery. He was formerly the owner, but following financial difficulties, which resulted in the closure of a number of mine shafts, the colliery was bought out by Scot Highlands.

Big Redface is extremely embarrassed. He had been aware of the existence of the disused shafts on his neighbour's land because they had been constructed during his ownership of the Colliery. He had not disclosed this fact to Lord Stretcher's engineers because the shafts had been built without permission, albeit abandoned soon thereafter. Furthermore, the Colliery had lost the plans so that he would have been unable in any event to identify their precise location.

Highlands and Big Redface have been advised that if the matter were to go to court, the Colliery would win: for, in law, persons who keep things on their land which are liable to escape, do so at their peril; for if there is an 'escape' and it causes damage, they will be found liable. However, Big Redface is concerned that the history of the old mine shafts would emerge in court and that he, and his employer Scot, could face huge further claims.

On the other hand, armed with his lawyer's advice, he knows that Scot will expect little short of full compensation and he needs to strive hard to come out of this mediation with a good settlement. A 'good settlement' would be in the region of £170,000, for Big Redface is aware that the loss of profits and wages claim is somewhat dubious – the Colliery had hit a bad patch and was likely to suffer losses and redundancies in any event. Whatever the settlement, it needs to be dressed up in a way that renders it 'palatable' to Scot Highlands.

Confidential brief: Lord Stretcher

Lord Stretcher is a wealthy landowner. He had a good reputation in the community, but the collapse of the reservoir has made him a 'laughing stock'. His engineers had wished to carry out a full survey upon finding the disused mine shafts, but Lord Stretcher had vetoed this: he wanted to cut costs and speed up the process so that the reservoir could be up and running in time to capitalize upon the anticipated summer water shortages. Furthermore, he is not sure whether his predecessors built the shafts and the passages, for he has lost the deeds to the property.

He has been advised by his lawyers that there is absolute liability for damage caused by things stored upon the property: for in law, persons who keep things on their land which are liable to escape, do so at their peril; and if there is an 'escape' and it causes damage, they will be found liable.

Lord Stretcher therefore does not wish to go to court. Apart from losing the case, he would not want his greed and incompetence to be disclosed and further aired in public. His own costs are more than likely to be met by insurance anyway. He would thus be prepared to pay in order to achieve a settlement, provided the payment were kept confidential, and there is a full admission of liability by the Colliery. In any event, the Colliery's claim is grossly inflated and he would look equally foolish in the eyes of Scot and 'Big' if he were seen to pay out huge sums. He would consider he had 'got away with it' if he were to achieve a private settlement in the sum of £50,000.

Psychological Commentary

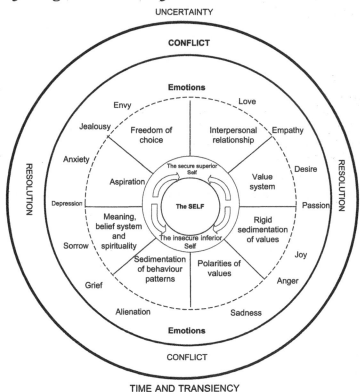

Figure 4 Wheels of emotions. The diagram represents a non-chronological and non-linear interconnection of some of the existential givens.

The wheel in Figure 4 demonstrates the concept of the secure and insecure Self rotating through Emotions, all within the limitations of some of the givens, such as Uncertainty and Time. Two aspects are now added: Freedom of Choice and Aspirations and Meanings. This psychological commentary will consider how these are all interconnected and will attempt to show how they are manifested in this Case Study.

Emotions

The role of emotions in mediation cannot be overemphasized. Every emotion is connected with the givens, and each emotion is a manifestation of an aspect of people's world-view. Indeed, emotions are most useful tools for the mediator and for the parties to gain a further insight into aspects of their own world-view. More importantly, they can highlight some of the ambivalences that each party holds and which may have originally lead them into the dispute. That is their ambiguity: they 'want but cannot get'.

Emotions are frequently ascribed a negative connotation and often suppressed: there is a perception that transgressions and misdeeds may be committed through uncontrolled emotions. Yet every emotion has its own function and can be viewed from both a positive and a negative perspective. Emotions can represent a state of being or a trait in an individual. If Lord Stretcher is described as an angry individual, that is a personal trait; if he is described as being angry, that may be simply a transient state, a reaction to certain prevailing conditions (Lazarus 1991), possibly precipitated by Mr Redface or even the mediator. This book is concerned only with emotions that occur as transient states, during the process of mediation.

INTERACTION OF DIFFERENT EMOTIONS

Psychologists have attempted to classify and define emotions: Richard Lazarus, in *Emotion and Adaptation* (1991) analyses a cluster of some 135 emotions. He does not define each emotion precisely, for each single emotion is perpetually attached, linked and inter-acting with some other emotion.

When Mr Redface expresses anger, he will also experience a vast number of other emotions: jealousy, envy, hostility, bitterness, hate and vindictiveness may all be part of the initial emotion, for they are all interconnected. The mediator is not concerned with defining precisely each particular emotion; he or she needs to appreciate that emotion, whether on its own or in conjunction with other emotions, is not a negative factor; rather it may facil-itate the exploration and understanding of Lord Stretcher's and Mr Redface's world-view.

PEOPLE ARE NEVER WITHOUT EMOTIONS

Emotions are always present in every aspect and at every stage of our consciousness (Sartre 1958). Similarly in mediation: even if neither Lord Stretcher nor Mr Redface express emotion, emotions will nevertheless be present. The desire to conceal emotions is an equally strong emotion. Any suggestion by Lord Stretcher or Mr Redface that 'I am not emotional' would be capable of profound challenge.

EMOTIONS INVARIABLY DENOTE SOMETHING

The knowledge that emotions invariably 'denote something' is another crucial factor for the mediator to take on board. When Mr Redface demonstrates an emotion, it is always directed some-where or at something – it will never be in isolation. His emotions are therefore an ideal vehicle through which the mediator can interpret parts of Mr Redface's world-view. This in turn will illu-minate Redface's values, rigid sedimentations, the construct of his self-esteem, as well as his true motivations and aspirations in the dispute. Disclosure of emotions will also reveal the object of those emotions, whether it be anger or frustration or joy: they will reveal *what* it is that is making Mr Redface angry, what is the *cause* of his frustration, or the *source* of his joy. And whether they are aware of it or not, both Lord Stretcher and Mr Redface will constantly disclose their values through their emotions. The mediator's capacity and skill to listen to and to recognize emotions thus plays a vital role in facilitating the process.

Take, for example, a scenario in which Lord Stretcher were to lose his temper, or develop an excessive rage, whether at Mr Redface's attitude or towards the mediator. The mediator might need to do the following: firstly he might wish to explore his own immediate reaction, as the mediator needs to deal with his own desire to protect himself. He can use the technique of simply breathing to allow a moment of reflection. Then he must try to put himself into Lord Stretcher's shoes. By reflecting back and acknowledging what Lord Stretcher has said, the mediator can demonstrate his own understanding of the emotions that Lord Stretcher is experiencing. This may assuage much of Lord Stretcher's anger, as he will feel he has been heard. It is also likely to elicit further information as to *why* he is so angry – whether he feels slighted, or even cheated. This in turn may well lead to Lord Stretcher expounding upon his reputation in the community, thereby revealing that the dispute may have little to do with money.

Mediators can frequently be unsettled by undue displays of emotion. Raised voices, violent gestures and other manifestations of rage can be alarming; weeping, sobbing and the flow of tears can be discomforting. Yet it may be seen from the above that mediators should in fact welcome such outbursts, and appreciate that they render the mediator's task a little easier than if the parties remain wholly unemotional throughout. It is through the emotions displayed by Lord Stretcher and Mr Redface that the mediator will be able to acquire a substantial insight into their values and value systems.

Freedom of choice
All individuals exert the freedom to make various choices, within the constraints and limitations imposed upon them by the conditions of the world. Sartre argues that the very fact of being in the

world is a manifestation of freedom of choice. 'Even if we do not choose, we have chosen' (1958: 632).

In mediation, there are always numerous choices. Lord Stretcher may feel ashamed or humiliated at the collapse of his reservoir but, whereas he cannot change that fact, he at least has the choice of changing his attitude towards it. He could after all accept it; he could even look at it from a positive viewpoint; or alternatively he can remain embarrassed and dishonoured by it (*see* Strasser and Strasser 1997).

The ability to exercise this freedom to choose is of vital importance in mediation. Both Lord Stretcher and Mr Redface have the ability to choose a 'good enough' solution. When, towards the end of the mediation, they are negotiating a final compromise, whether in terms of compensation or some other solution, this element of choice of a 'good enough' resolution to the dispute will become an essential factor which may need to be emphasized by the mediator.

Aspirations and meanings
'Meaning' is a vital tool for human survival. The psychiatrist, Victor Frankl, developed this premise as a Holocaust survivor, demonstrating that those who encapsulated meaning in their lives, whether spiritual, ideological or simply by telling the story of the Holocaust, increased their chances of survival over those without meaning.

Meaning is interconnected with our values, our aspirations and our strategies for survival in life. While both Lord Stretcher and Mr Redface will have developed their own meanings in their own way, neither can escape the process of searching for a meaning in life, and therefore in the dispute facing them. Both will have been affected by cultural and family influences, but each is responsible and can add to or subtract from the cultural influences so as to lead an authentic life, based on his own assumptions.

Meanings and aspirations are very much connected with self-esteem, in that aspirations are created in order to maintain self-esteem. It would be helpful for the mediator to know, for example, whether Lord Stretcher's 'meanings' in life hinge upon acquiring and maintaining wealth, or achieving and protecting status, or demonstrating principled behaviour towards others? Similarly with Mr Redface's aspirations: are they aimed at simply making money; or being popular with his peers and subordinates, or purely at always being in the right? The question that will ultimately arise in this mediation is to what degree Lord Stretcher's or Mr Redface's meanings are rigidly embedded in their value and behaviour systems. Are they able to change or vary the degree of their aspirations and meanings to a more acceptable level while still maintaining their self-esteem?

Practical and Procedural Commentary

Introduction
This Case Study is similarly based on a classic legal authority: *Rylands v Fletcher* (1868) LR 3HL 330. This case, again encountered by most law students in their first year of legal studies, established the principle that a person who collects and keeps anything on his land which is likely to 'do mischief' if it escapes is prima facie answerable for any damage caused as a natural consequence of the escape.

The Case Study provides a suitable background for the role players to embroider and accentuate a number of familiar conflict situations:

- the big and powerful versus the small and vulnerable
- the 'landed gentry' versus the 'salt of the earth' labourer
- the landowner with inherited wealth versus the 'hard grafter' who worked his way up from nothing
- the party with a high reputation to maintain and protect
- parties with 'skeletons in the cupboard' – which could materialize if the matter went to court
- a party who needs to impress his superior with a 'good' settlement

- a party who has been advised that he has a cast-iron case in law

Trainee difficulties with the skills

The students work on this Case Study at approximately the half-way stage of the course. It often marks a turning point – where the participants begin to shed their 'old' approach to dispute resolution, and proceed to a new and fresh style of communication. The methods and techniques to which they have hitherto been accustomed or conditioned, whether as a result of their professional training, their upbringing or the daily environment in which they live, are not easily relinquished. The instinctive confrontational interventions, the conditioned adversarial responses and the judgmental attitudes, still rise to the surface intermittently; but the participants are beginning to learn that these are nearly always inappropriate and less than effective in mediation. As these conditioned traits begin to diminish, a new, more open and empathic style is slowly initiated.

This new style, however, is still employed in a *mechanical* way. The participants remain very self-conscious; they are still *mock*-mediating rather than genuinely experiencing the process. They are consciously and visibly having to remind themselves to:

- 'actively' listen
- maintain reasonable eye contact where appropriate
- use silence and other non-verbal communication (nodding, etc.)
- paraphrase
- 'reflect back'
- summarize
- be mindful of posture and 'body language'

Yet an interesting and common feature is that the participants tend to form an attachment to one or other technique – and use it to excess. So for example, the following is not unusual amongst the trainee mediators:

- excessive use of silence:
  long, uncomfortable, embarrassing and unnatural periods of
  silence after almost every exchange, with the trainee mediator
  fixing the party with an unswerving stare in order to maintain
  continuous eye contact
- endless summarizing:
  summaries following each point that is made, when there is
  hardly anything to summarize
- constant paraphrasing:
  every other sentence or utterance made by the party is repeated
  in the participant's words
- unnatural mirroring of posture:
  artificial attempts at copying the body language of the party –
  crossing legs when the party crosses their legs, folding arms
  when they do so, leaning forward, leaning back, putting hands
  behind the head, and so on

The participant has discovered a particular technique, whether
the power of silence, or the effect of summarizing, and is deter-
mined to utilize it as frequently as possible.

It is at this stage of the course that the students frequently
experience difficulties with a number of the skills set out in
Chapter 3 (Communication Skills). Some of these skills and the
inherent problems in employing them can now usefully be considered in the context of this Case Study.

Acceptance

This skill involves accepting a party's expression or statement at
face value and in a wholly non-judgmental way. The use of this
skill is often highlighted by this Case Study and by the robust way
in which the role-players invariably play the part of Lord Stretcher.
Take, for example, the situation where Lord Stretcher says to the
mediator:

I know that the House of Lords have ruled that a person in my
position who floods neighbouring land is automatically liable,

but the House of Lords were wrong – they are a bunch of idiots and when I get to court I will prove that to the judge who tries this case.

The lawyer-trained mediator's instinctive response might be reminiscent of a famous 1981 tennis player's retort: 'You cannot be serious!' or perhaps a more measured: 'Surely you do not believe that the judge will ignore a House of Lords' decision?' or even 'You will have great difficulty achieving that!'

The mediator would be well advised to reflect upon the effect that such responses would have upon a party such as Lord Stretcher. Would it assist in building a rapport? Would it create that level of trust that will enable Lord Stretcher to reveal his underlying fears and concerns about going to court? Is it likely to persuade Lord Stretcher to change his opinion of the strength of his case and his prospects of success?

Acceptance means accepting that this is Lord Stretcher's view, that this is 'where he is coming from', and accepting that, from *his* perspective, it is an entirely valid, logical and reasonable stance to take. The lawyers in particular on the course find this one of the most difficult concepts to appreciate. Their training and experience has taught them to analyse all that they hear; to dissect and evaluate every piece of information, to view all facts and figures in their particular context and to put all data into its proper and correct perspective. Consequently, when they are met head-on with a proposition from one party, which is an affront to their logical perceptions, they instinctively seek to challenge, confront and contest.

The psychotherapeutically trained mediator on the other hand, will acknowledge and welcome this demonstration of Lord Stretcher's world-view and will be eager to explore it further. The following are examples of how a sensitive mediator might respond to such demonstration:

How do you think the House of Lords should have decided that case?

What aspect of that case do you think will demonstrate most
strongly to the trial judge that the House of Lords was wrong?
How do you see your responsibilities as a neighbour?
What do you see as your duties in preventing damage to your
neighbour's property?
How do you think Big Redface sees the position, as a person
whose neighbour has caused damage to his property?

This might oblige Lord Stretcher to vocalize his justification
for his extreme stance, and might thereby enable him to hear, from
his own mouth, the ambiguity of his position. If a position can be
reached where Lord Stretcher is persuaded to view the issues from
his neighbour's perspective, a true foundation for a settlement has
been laid. This would probably not have been achieved by confronting Lord Stretcher with the absurdity of his propositions, but
might have merely served to entrench him further in his obstinate
position.

Empathy and sympathy

By the stage at which the participants tackle the Highlands v
Stretcher Case Study, they have been made fully aware that
'empathy' is a vital and significant element in a mediator's
armoury. But distinguishing that from sympathy is not without its
complications. The following example from Lord Stretcher's case
may illustrate some of the problems encountered. Lord Stretcher
is telling the mediator in private caucus about the effect this dispute has had upon him:

It has been terrible. My reputation has sunk to unimaginable
depths. I cannot walk into the local pub without people moving away. They cross the road when they see me approach. I have
even been spat upon by children in the village . . .

A *sympathetic* reaction by the mediator would be to say something like: 'Lord Stretcher, how appalling – that's despicable
behaviour, certainly on the part of the children, it must have made
you feel absolutely awful.'

The trained mediator will avoid such a response, and would seek to convey a more *empathic* message such as: 'Lord Stretcher, I can see how extremely upsetting that must have been for you.'

By showing that he or she has heard, acknowledged and understood Lord Stretcher's situation, the mediator can maintain his or her trust and continue to build a rapport. At the same time, he or she will remain sufficiently independent so as to be able effectively to move the process forward to a resolution. The danger of showing sympathy is that Lord Stretcher will believe that the mediator has been swayed to his side, persuaded to *agree* with the merits of his case over and above that of Mr Redface. The result can be potentially disastrous:

> Why are you trying to get me to see the position from Redface's point of view? In the last caucus you *agreed* with me as to how appalling this situation was – I thought you were on my side!

There will be occasions when Lord Stretcher or Mr Redface may be overtly seeking sympathy:

> What was I to do?
> What can I do now?
> Can you imagine what it was like for me?
> Can't you see how terrible this situation is for me?

In such circumstances, the mediator's skills will be tested to the limit, and the temptation to 'jump into the ditch' will be powerful – but should be resisted at all costs. The risks of being perceived as colluding or siding with one party over the other – whichever side holds the perception – can be fatal to the success of the mediation process.

On the other hand, certain expressions of empathy can equally be used inappropriately. Take, for example, a medical negligence dispute where the Claimant has been left totally paraplegic: in such a situation a mediator's response of : 'I can understand how you feel' would, not unreasonably, be met with: 'Of course you *can't* understand how I feel – nobody can understand how I feel or what I have to go through!' As in all matters, the mediator must use balance and discretion.

Identifying themes

In Lord Stretcher's case, the theme most frequently bubbling to the surface is that of 'reputation'. Thus, the role-players will make statements at various stages of the caucus, possibly not even consciously aware that they are repeating a theme:

> I am very well known and respected in the area, you know...
> This has made me a laughing stock in the village ...
> We have been the landowners here for centuries, and our name is now mud ...
> I used to be looked up to and esteemed as a benefactor to the community...

The astute mediator would readily recognize that there is a recurring theme here, which reveals that Lord Stretcher's reputation is one of his prime concerns. An effective and appropriate way to deal with this might, for example, be as follows:

> What I am hearing from you is that your standing in the community is very much an important factor for you ...

or

> I can understand that you have always been highly regarded in this community and so your reputation means a great deal to you ...

and then perhaps

> So how would your reputation be affected if we were not to reach a settlement?

By recognizing that a theme is recurring in this way, the mediator can ensure that Lord Stretcher feels heard on an issue that may be of fundamental importance to him. This will enable the mediator to work with Lord Stretcher in a more productive way.

Handling lawyers, experts and others

Finally, in this Case Study, Lord Stretcher has a solicitor present. The trainee mediator is thus presented with the further problem of dealing with the additional factor of a lawyer's input at the mediation.

Curiously, when role-playing the part of the lawyer, the participants invariably adopt a role of someone who is difficult, obstreperous and constantly interfering with and obstructing the process:

> Just a moment, Lord Stretcher, I don't think we can go as far as that . . .
>
> Can I just have a word with my client before we leave this issue . . .
>
> I don't think that's a fair question to put to my client . . .
>
> Have you put that to Big Redface as well, because I think you should . . .
>
> We are not prepared to concede anything in relation to liability at this stage . . .
>
> I don't think you need answer that, Lord Stretcher . . .

This is not the experience generally of parties to real mediations. Lawyers are frequently as anxious for a settlement as their client. They often have a joint interest in a successful outcome. They will probably have needed to persuade their client to participate and so the outcome – success or failure – will very much reflect back upon them. But it is worthwhile noting that the perception of the participants of lawyers as 'rottweilers' – aggressive, tenacious, uncompromising and unyielding – possibly reflects that of litigants, prospective litigants and many of the public.

But what if the lawyer – or the expert, or the partner or friend who has come along to support – is aggressive, tenacious, uncompromising and unyielding, and takes an obstructive approach towards the mediation? If Mr Redface's lawyer has advised him that they have a 'cast-iron' case, any compromise or concession on the part of Mr Redface in the mediation may be seen as a 'vote of no confidence' in the lawyer. Or the expert may have insisted that his opinion, his diagnosis or prognosis, his evaluation or assessment in Lord Stretcher's case is wholly reliable and accurate. Equally in that case, any conciliation or surrender of ground will be seen as an expression of doubt in him as an expert. So too with partners and relatives, who may have a hope of financial benefit from the outcome and consequently may be urging the party not to give way or not to accept less than the maximum possible.

How does the mediator treat such parties at the mediation?

The 'overriding objective' must always be to gain trust and build rapport – with each and every person round the table. The mediator must not allow a wedge to be driven between him or herself and *any* of the parties. The lawyer, the expert and the relative must all be brought 'on side' and into the working alliance that is hopefully being created.

If this cannot be achieved within the caucuses or the joint sessions, the mediator may feel obliged to consider separating the party from the lawyer, expert or relative. There are no hard and fast rules on this and each occasion will require a judgment call on the part of the mediator. It may need to be done only if the mediator has formed a clear impression that the presence of the other person is not conducive to progress towards settlement, or is in some way hindering the creation of a proper environment for compromise. Nevertheless, it must always be done sensitively and considerately, so that any understanding and confidence between the lawyer or expert and the mediator is not put at risk. The mediator should always be perceptive to the possibility that the litigant will feel 'denuded' by the absence of their lawyer, and that the lawyer, expert or relative will be offended by any sense of exclusion.

The mediator will need to consider a formula of words in such circumstances, possibly something along the following lines:

Just as it is helpful for me to see both parties separately, it may also be helpful for me to see you [the lawyer, etc.] separately as well.

I feel that if I can get each of your views on this separately, it might help to give me a fuller and clearer picture of the issues . . .

Perhaps if we were to meet briefly separately, it might enable each of you to speak frankly and openly, so that this can be taken forward more quickly . . .

May I suggest that I speak to each of you individually, simply as part of the normal mediation process . . .

Some mediators prefer to lay the foundation for such a course right at the outset, in their opening address to all the parties in the joint session, for example:

I may wish to see each of you individually in separate private caucus sessions as the mediation unfolds. This would be perfectly normal and is my usual approach in such matters, so nobody need feel uneasy about it.

Whatever the situation, the issue of the 'difficult', obstinate, intractable or awkward party at the mediation must be addressed by the mediator and should not allowed to be swept under the carpet.

11

Case Study 4

The Misleading Banker's Reference
Heavenly Burn v Hell, Err & Partners –
A Second Time!

Practical and Procedural Commentary

This Case Study is mediated twice, the second occasion being towards the latter end of the course. The second occasion is often used as a second half of an adjourned or two-day mediation, so as to give the students on the course an opportunity to experience taking up a mediation from a mid-point and pursuing it to conclusion.

On this second occasion, however, one altered 'scenario' is that there is a staged 'walk-out' by one of the parties: the participant taking the role of Mr Heavenly is instructed to stage an angry 'scene' and walk out during the opening joint session.

At first sight, mediating the same case again within a short space of time on the same course might appear a futile or worthless exercise. The mediator will probably have discovered the hidden agenda – or agendas – set out in the confidential briefs of one or more of the parties; he or she will be aware, or may recall some of the better or more penetrating questions to ask; he or she may feel that the pitfalls encountered on the first occasion can easily be avoided.

These observations may be correct, but they do not affect the considerable benefit that is derived by the participants from mediating the same case for a second time. The participants are instructed to concentrate on the *process* and the employment of the various skills learned, rather than seeking a resolution. In this way, the participants learn to:

- recognize that two dispute situations will never be exactly the same when personalities are involved (even where the same participants play the roles again)
- separate the dispute from the facts and the facts from the people
- appreciate the importance of approaching a dispute situation with an open mind and without preconceived ideas or assumptions
- 'bracket' and put to the back of one's mind any information gathered or acquired on the previous occasion when the Case Study was mediated
- that an effective question in one mediation or dispute situation may be wholly ineffective or inappropriate in a slightly different situation or in another circumstance
- that there are no specific rules which can be applied to mediations even where the nature of the dispute may be identical
- each mediation will throw up differing problems involving individual 'judgment calls'

The 'walk-out'

The participant taking the role of Mr Heavenly is directed to stage the walk-out at the conclusion of the opening statement by Mr Hell. Even where this mediation takes the form of 'Day 2' of a two-day mediation, it is likely that the mediator would commence by conducting a joint session, simply to remind the parties of certain aspects of the process, and to allow the parties to express any further thoughts they have had in the interim.

The purpose of the walk-out exercise is to present the trainee mediator with his or her first encounter of 'raw emotion'. If Heavenly plays the part well, he or she will become increasingly agitated during Hell's opening statement. Having been instructed by the mediator that the opening statements are to be allowed to proceed without interruption, Heavenly can only remain silently fuming, until he or she erupts in anger and frustration, and begins to storm out of the room.

Taken by surprise, the trainee mediators display a wide variety of reactions. Some are quite dumbfounded and they remain fixed to their seats, unable to move or speak, watching impotently while Heavenly disappears angrily out of the door. Eventually, they may rise to their feet and shuffle embarrassingly out of the door in search of the disappearing party, while mumbling some uncomfortable apology to the mortified parties left sitting in the room.

Others take a much more 'robust' line: 'Come back here and sit down!' or even worse:

Where do you think you're going – come back at once!
Don't be so impatient – just wait – your turn will come!
That's extremely rude of you – just sit down and allow the process to continue!
That's not very helpful, now, is it?!
Let's just calm down, shall we?!
This is not going to get us anywhere, now, is it?!

Some have even tried to reinforce their 'schoolteacher' approach by rushing to the door and standing spread-eagled against it, physically preventing Heavenly from leaving the room.

The mediator should bear two things in mind if he or she is to tackle such a situation sensitively and effectively:

1. Anger is an emotion which can swiftly provide an insight into a substantial part of the world-view of the party expressing it. As seen in the section on Emotions in the third Case Study, the mediator should be neither dismayed nor apprehensive at such a display of emotion. It is something positive and concrete, a phenomenon with which he or she,

as a psychotherapeutically trained mediator, should be eager to grapple and work.

and

2. The mediator is seeking to build a rapport with the party and to create a bond of trust. Showing irritation or frustration or even disappointment at the behaviour of one side will merely destroy any real chance of such trust or rapport being formed.

So what is the optimum approach of a mediator in such a situation? Empathy is very much the essence of the answer. A sensitive and effective mediator will demonstrate empathy and understanding, and thereby help to diffuse the anger and the emotion.

> I can see that you are very angry and I can understand that this must be very distressing for you ...
> It is understandably very frustrating for you to hear ...
> I realize how significantly this must affect you ...
> You are obviously terribly angry and distressed by all this ...
> I appreciate how much this is upsetting you ...

Such expressions of empathy may possibly assist in defusing some of the extreme heat and emotion in the situation, but the mediator still needs to persuade the party to resume the process and stay in the mediation. Words of encouragement can frequently help to succeed in this objective, something along the following lines:

> I am confident that we can achieve movement if you just bear with me a little longer ...
> By all means you are free to leave, for this is a voluntary process, but now that we are all here, let's just see whether, by giving it a chance, something might come of it ...
> You have been good enough to attend and to participate in this mediation, I am sure some progress can be made if we just give it a bit longer ...

> It can be a very frustrating process, but the statistics of successful resolutions are very high, so why don't we see whether we can move forward a little . . .
>
> We will shortly be speaking together in private in the caucus session, and you will then have every opportunity to express your feelings to me fully and frankly . . .

Such exchanges should ideally be conducted in private and not in front of the other parties. The mediator should ideally make a short explanation to the remaining parties, stating that he or she will just have a quick word with Heavenly, before returning as soon as possible. Then, taking Heavenly to one side, the mediator can speak freely without fear or concern as to what the other parties may overhear.

On returning to the joint session, it is vital for the mediator to be sensitive to the resulting emotions of both parties. Heavenly will be understandably embarrassed that

a) he allowed himself to lose his temper/control in front of the other side, and

b) despite all that, he has been persuaded to return, and may therefore be seen to have 'backed down'

Mr Hell, in the meantime may have experienced some discomfort at this display of emotion and lack of control, and will feel uncomfortable when the process resumes. Alternatively, he may be pleased that Mr Heavenly has 'shown himself to the mediator in his true colours', and will hope that this will have influenced the mediator in his favour. Again, some soothing words of encouragement – if possible without being patronizing, (although this can be difficult) – may help to retrieve the situation:

> Heavenly has very kindly agreed to remain in the mediation and is willing to give it a further chance . . .
>
> I think it is helpful if we can all appreciate that this is an emotional time, and we are all bound to feel some frustration during the course of the day . . .

It can sometimes be beneficial to the process for both sides to express their emotions freely, for it can help me as the mediator to understand the level of feeling on each side . . .

Finally, an 'outburst' of emotion like that can give the mediator a fruitful entrée to the next caucus, with whichever party:

With Heavenly
Can you tell me a little more about what it was that made you feel angry?

This ought to provide a very fertile line of enquiry and exploration, for it could reveal – or lead to the revelation of – the very core of the dispute.

And with Hell
What did you make of Heavenly's reaction to your opening statement?

Or
What do you think it was that made Heavenly so angry?

This might not only start the process of encouraging one party to see the dispute through the eyes of the other – always an extremely powerful tool in dispute resolution – but may also usefully reveal one party's true perception of the other party's case.

Breaking deadlock

Assume that Lord Stretcher and Mr Redface have reached deadlock. Most experienced mediators will have experienced this stage in a mediation, often described as 'the wall', where intransigence on the part of one or more of the parties has led to an apparent and complete impasse. It is the point where frustration at the ostensible lack of progress will lead to rising tempers, increasing exchange of accusations of a progressively more personal nature and a total disillusionment with the mediation process – as well as possibly the mediator.

There may be a large number of factors at play, contributing to this unfortunate position. Either Mr Redface or Lord Stretcher may be shielding behind 'matters of principle', or their respective lawyers, experts or other supporters may be exercising an unduly protective influence. 'Office politics', family or community pressures, company policy, corporate or internal rivalry or hostility, animosity between colleagues – these may all be influences affecting the strategy adopted by the parties, rendering them unwilling or unable to move from their entrenched positions. There are a number of steps a mediator can take in such situations, as set out below:

Change of approach

The mediator can attempt a different approach, and vary the methods adopted thus far. These can include:

- taking a break
- taking a walk with one or more of the parties, or suggesting that all get some fresh air
- seeing the lawyers or experts or other parties separately
- suggesting that lawyers or experts get together
- discussing the position in a joint session and 'brainstorming' a solution
- setting a deadline for the end of the mediation

'Reframing' the problem

The mediator might try to re-present the problem or the area of dispute, or the 'sticking point', in a different light:

- focusing on each party's needs and interests
- re-phrasing arguments in a 'principled' rather than 'positional' form
- lateral thought applied to the problem or 'thinking out of the box' may bring fruitful ideas for the parties to consider

- settlement could be sought on more minor or peripheral issues, such as for example the compensation for the lost wages of the Redface Colliery workers. With some level of agreement achieved, a momentum towards full settlement might be initiated

Being positive
While being positive may sometimes be detrimental to a party's self-esteem if the impasse cannot be broken, the mediator may nevertheless seek to reassure the parties by encouraging them to examine the positive aspects of the mediation, in the hope that this will imbue them with further patience, commitment and energy. Thus the mediator might:

- identify and highlight, if possible, the positive side of any the negative elements
- remind the parties of the achievements or movements in the mediation thus far
- inform the parties that such impasse is not unusual
- remind the parties of the high rate of success in mediations

and above all

- remain calm and hopeful!

12

Case Study 5

The Case of the Defective Flooring
Junior Crooks Ltd v Cheeky Ltd

The facts

Junior Crooks Ltd (JC) are a moderately successful book publishing company, specializing in children's educational books.
They entered into a contract with Kract & Giveway Building Co.
(KGB) for the construction of a new prestigious factory and book-
production plant at a site in Wales.

Within a month of the building construction being virtually
complete, cracks began to appear in the floor of the factory. Three
months later, large sections of the floor had 'lifted' from the concrete base. The floor had been laid by Cheeky Ltd a specialist
flooring subcontractor. They had used a technique involving the
laying of two coats of a magnesium oxychloride composition on a
screeded concrete base. Cheeky argued that the new flooring had
been properly laid, but this particular type of floor required
careful and continuous maintenance. They contend that this was
fully explained to JC's architects, but the required maintenance
had clearly not been implemented. JC deny any fault and have
issued a claim against Cheeky Ltd as follows:

Replacement flooring (including investigative treatment)	£ 53,000
Storage of books and machinery during remedial works	£ 3,000
Lost wages to employees during remedial works	£ 90,000
Loss of profit during temporary closure	£ 45,000
Fixed overheads producing no returns	£ 16,000
	£207,000

Cheeky Ltd are defending the claim on the grounds that (i) in law they do not have a contract with JC and thus owe a contractual duty *only* to the main contractors KGB; and (ii) JC caused the cracking by their failure to maintain.

In view of the cost of litigation and the urgency of the situation, both parties have agreed to mediation. The mediation will be attended by Don Panic, Chief Executive of JC, and by Major Stress, a director of Cheeky Ltd.

Confidential Brief: Don Panic (on behalf of Junior Crooks Ltd)

Don Panic is the Chief Executive of JC and is attending the mediation on their behalf. He was aware of detailed instructions given by Cheeky Ltd for the maintenance of the flooring, but had been concerned by the cost and labour intensiveness involved. Don Panic discussed it with his architects and they concluded that it might be possible to cut down on certain aspects of maintenance. However, the architects advised Panic that, as few people knew the full effects of the new magnesium oxychloride floor composition, cutting down on maintenance could be a risk. Despite this warning, Don Panic had issued fresh and limited instructions on maintenance to his staff.

When cracks appeared in the flooring, Don Panic began to panic. The factory had been built so that it could be the venue for the 50th International Book Fair, hosted by Junior Crooks Ltd. The grand opening of the factory was to coincide with the opening of the Book Fair. Huge profits were forecast as a result of hosting the Book Fair, and the future of the company would be assured. As construction of the factory had started well in time, Don Panic had not informed KGB of the deadline, and time had not been made 'of the essence'. [The Mediator has not yet been told of the Book Fair issue.]

Panic has made enquiries in the construction industry, but no other flooring contractor is prepared to take on remedial works to this type of flooring, and complete replacement could not be carried out in time. If Cheeky were able to reinstate the flooring in time for the opening, Panic is authorized to forgo substantial parts of JC's claim. The losses resulting in a cancellation of the Book Fair at their factory would spell ruin for the company, whereas the profits from such a Fair would well exceed their losses. Don Panic's reputation in the company is at stake. He feels responsible for the cracking floor, and therefore must try to recoup the losses so as to be seen to 'succeed' in the mediation.

Confidential Brief: Major Stress (on behalf of Cheeky Ltd)

Major Stress joined the Research and Development department of Cheeky Ltd some 8 years ago after a successful career in the Army Engineering Corps. Within a short time of arriving at Cheeky Ltd, Major Stress had pioneered a new technique of flooring using a compound of magnesium oxychloride, which created a superb-looking finish while being extremely hard wearing. However, the technique required very precise 'curing and dressing' procedures: the compound needed to be very carefully mixed in accurate proportions; it could not be laid if the mix was unduly 'wet'; and the top coat needed to be carefully measured so as to be of sufficient thickness to prevent cracking. Furthermore, once laid, the flooring required continuous maintenance by damp-mopping and polishing.

Unfortunately, the 'curing and dressing' procedures were proving too complex for the average building site worker and the maintenance regime was also obviously too arduous to be properly imposed by building owners. Consequently a number of new floors laid by Cheeky Ltd were now experiencing problems. Cheeky Ltd are prepared to carry out remedial works for JC, but are neither prepared nor able to pay out large sums in compensation. Sales have been significantly hit and their work force is already overstretched dealing with complaints of defective flooring.

Major Stress is under severe stress. He knows that he pioneered a masterful product and that, with a little time, the procedures could have been perfected. A substantial claim from JC would result in Cheeky going into voluntary liquidation; he would lose the opportunity to 'prove' his product and vindicate his reputation, as well as that of the company. He therefore needs to skilfully negotiate a very substantial reduction in JC's claim.

Psychological Commentary

Interaction of all psychological aspects

In this commentary, the interaction of the various psychological aspects and ingredients of the mediation process will be considered in the context of the dispute between Junior Crooks Ltd and Cheeky Ltd.

In the diagrammatical 'wheel' below, and in all the others, the self has always been central, but moving or shifting through all the other aspects. Although the 'Self' is in some respects at the centre of any analysis of the psychological aspects of conflict, this does not mean that the exploration of the self is more important than the exploration of any other aspect. Thus any other part of the wheel might equally be considered 'central': the exploration of a party's value system or their choices is not to be considered of secondary importance. All are interconnected and none are in a chronological or linear order.

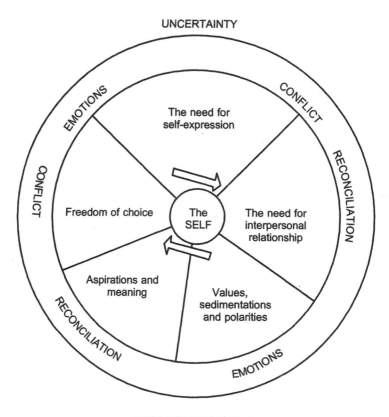

Figure 5 Aspects of conflict.
The diagram represents a non-chronological and non-linear interconnection of some of the existential givens.

Although it might appear that nearly every part of human conduct or behaviour hinges upon the self and self-esteem, in practice virtually all our actions are performed in an interwoven web. All our endeavours are directed towards the protection of our 'self', to safeguard our self-image, to achieve our aims and aspirations. Through our need for self-expression, we develop interpersonal relationships, while at the same time forging our values and meanings in response to the limitations and givens of the world, such as uncertainty and the transiency of time. This generates our world-view, and governs our choices and our ability in conflict situations to choose a 'good enough' solution.

Reputation – and all the issues of self-esteem that accompany it – again rear their heads in this case study and provide the trainee mediator and the role players with a welcome variety of themes to explore. For Major Stress, this floor is his creation, his 'baby', and any criticism of it is easily taken personally, as an affront to his professionalism. The claim by Junior Crooks is thus potentially fatal to Major Stress's reputation, for not only will it affect his existing status and standing within his company, but with the probable demise of Cheeky Ltd as a flooring company in consequence, he will be prevented from recovering or enhancing his reputation further in the future. So self-esteem again plays a crucial part in the emotions and strategies of the parties – and a fertile area for the mediator to deal with as the mediation unfolds.

A skilful mediator may be able to discern much of Major Stress's values and value system from the assertions he makes about his career: he had a highly successful career in the Army Engineering Corps where he pioneered the development of a new type of flooring. The mediator may be able to recognize from this that his self-esteem may to some extent hinge upon being an innovator who produced a work of genius in the flooring product. His reputation and its preservation are therefore paramount and the money aspect of the dispute is a secondary consideration.

For Don Panic, uncertainty and time play an important part in this Case Study. He has the forthcoming Book Fair looming over the entire dispute. The ability to host the Book Fair at the given time appears to have taken over his entire meaning in life: to hold the Fair will result in huge profits for the company and thus greatly boost his reputation and enhance his self-esteem; to lose the opportunity would result in devastation for the company, a destruction of his image, and therefore a collapse of his self-esteem.

But does Don Panic's entire self-image and self-worth hinge upon the Book Fair, or can the mediator extrapolate other meanings and values in his life, which might facilitate a settlement? If the floor cannot be replaced in time, Don Panic has the freedom to choose his attitude and approach to an inexorable problem.

The continuing cycle of conflict and reconciliation is also an important element in this case study, for reconciliation would be extremely beneficial to both parties: Major Stress would benefit from a further opportunity to prove the worth of his product, and Don Panic would profit from the re-laying of his floor. Such a solution would require a degree of cooperation between the parties, and this might only be achieved if they can transcend their adversarial stance and enter into a working alliance. By exploring their respective value systems and their choices, and by gently confronting them with this paradox, the mediator may be in a position to facilitate a settlement that is not only acceptable but also profitable for both sides.

Practical and Procedural Commentary

Once again this Case Study is taken from a classic legal authority: *Junior Books Ltd v Veitchy Co Ltd* [1983] 1 AC 520. But it portrays a typical everyday situation of conflict in the consumer world: one party produces, sells and delivers a product which the other party claims to be defective. Each party makes allegations and counter-allegations of fault against the other. Neither party is prepared to back down. Both parties have a common commercial interest in a swift resolution of the dispute, yet they have both ended up in litigation. The case of *Junior Books Ltd v Veitchy Co Ltd*, as in the previous Case Studies, went from the High Court to the Court of Appeal and on to the House of Lords. Mediation might have been a great deal cheaper and would have provided a much swifter solution.

The mock mediation

This Case Study is one of the last mock mediations undertaken by the participants on the course. By this stage, they will have been taught all the basic skills and will have mediated in at least three mock mediations, as well as having participated in some twelve others as role-playing parties. Thus they will have experienced many of the pitfalls themselves, and seen many other participants manoeuvre their way in and out and around them, with varying degrees of success.

The main message to the participants at this phase of the course is to 'listen well – be natural – and be yourselves'. By truly listening to the role-playing parties, by allowing themselves to have a real and natural curiosity as to what they are being told by the parties, the trainee mediators learn to become less self-conscious, and less 'self-absorbed' with the fact that they are mediating.

At the end of the mock mediation, the trainee mediator's body posture is often most revealing: upon being told that 'time is up', their shoulders drop from being hunched and tense; a smile reappears on a previously stony and often expressionless face; and the body visibly 'opens' and relaxes. This quite clearly indicates that the student is still finding it an alien role in an unfamiliar process. The aim of the course is to create a natural ease, so that the participant feels comfortable as mediator, so that questions flow without the conscious endeavour of having to think of the next question and so that the techniques acquired are deployed naturally and effortlessly.

Challenging – and the 'catastrophic "what if" principle'

It is appropriate that in this last Case Study under discussion, we should consider the 'what if' principle. This involves a 'challenge' to the party, inviting them to re-assess and re-evaluate their expectations as well as their aims and aspirations, in the light of possible 'catastrophic' consequences. For example:

Major Stress, what effect would it have upon your reputation if this matter were to go to court and your flooring were to be heavily criticized?

How would you feel if your reputation were to be sullied?

Don Panic, what would happen if this floor is not ready for the Book Fair?

What would happen if your company feel you let them down?

By confronting the party with a 'worst-case scenario' the mediator provides them with an opportunity, within the mediation process and together with the mediator, to contemplate the worst that could happen. This will usually achieve one of two results:

- the party is able to re-evaluate their outlook upon the situation and possibly realize that the worst scenario 'might not be so bad after all' and that they could 'learn to live with it', thereby enabling a settlement to be secured at a 'good enough' level, even if lower than originally hoped for

or

- the party realizes that such a situation is 'too awful even to think about', thereby precipitating an upward shift from the originally held 'bottom-line' position

The question arises as to when it may be appropriate to deploy the 'catastrophic "what if" principle'. One view is that a challenge such as this is too confrontational to be used at an early stage in the mediation; and that such a challenge should be deployed almost as a last resort, when parties have adopted rigid stances and as a result have become deadlocked. Another view argues that a challenge to a party's values and outlook can be effectively employed at *any* stage in the process, provided it is used 'gently' or tentatively and with sensitivity.

In fact, it matters not at which point a challenge is used, *provided* the mediator has at that stage secured a sufficient level of trust and rapport. The likelihood is that in the early stages of the mediation, the mediator will not have had the opportunity to gain sufficient trust to be able to make such a challenge, without risking the disaffection of the party on the receiving end.

Getting to 'good enough'

A parallel concept to the 'what-if' principle is the 'good enough' principle. This enables the parties to re-evaluate and re-assess their aims and objectives so that they reach a point where they can state: 'This is good enough for me'. The effective mediator will aim to establish a realistic and appropriate level for each party's 'good enough' position; and the psychotherapeutically trained mediator may be best placed to achieve this.

Ethical issues

ASKING THE MEDIATOR TO BREACH CONFIDENCE

A common problem faced by mediators is how to deal with the question: What did the other side tell you when you were in caucus with them?

It is not unnatural that there should be a burning curiosity on the part of each party to ascertain what transpired in the caucus session with the opposing party. Each party will have experienced the style and manner of questioning from the mediator, and will be aware of what they themselves were persuaded to reveal as a result of the disarming skills of the mediator. So it is quite understandable that each party should be eager to discover what 'gems' the mediator has been able to extract from the other.

Sometimes it is more specific. An offer or proposal has been put to one side and the other party wants to know the reaction to it. All this will inevitably lead to invitations and exhortations to the mediator to breach confidence:

What did Don Panic say?
How did Major Stress react?
Have they said anything yet about . . .?
Has Major Stress indicated the level of compensation that he might pay?

What did Don Panic say about their maintenance regime?

Unless specifically permitted to do so, the mediator would be breaching the confidentiality of the caucus session were he or she to answer these questions by providing the information requested. It is vital that the mediator should not to be enticed into doing so: it cannot be repeated often enough, confidentiality is a cornerstone of mediation. It may be tempting for the mediator in his or her perpetual endeavour to create rapport by some overt attempt at collusion:

> Look, Major Stress, I'm going to let you into a secret – Don Panic does not know that I am telling you this but . . .

Were the mediator to reveal to Major Stress what was said in confidence by Don Panic, Major Stress could no longer have any real trust in the mediator: if the mediator is prepared to breach confidence in favour of one party then he or she may well do likewise in favour of the opposite party.

The student mediator is therefore taught to devise a personal form of words, or some formula or mode of explaining to parties why he or she cannot reveal what was said by the other side in private caucus. An example might be:

> I am sure you would not be happy if I were to disclose to them what has just been said between us and so, likewise, you will understand why I cannot reveal what transpired in my conversations with them.

The mediator must obviously recognize that deflecting questions in this way is a difficult task to carry out in a sensitive yet positive manner, as there will inevitably be an element of 'negative messaging' inherent in such a response. The party is bound to feel that the mediator is to some extent being evasive and simply deflecting a reasonable enquiry. In these circumstances, it is very useful to employ words of encouragement with which to accompany the 'negative' message:

... you will understand why I cannot reveal what transpired in my conversations with them. But I can tell you that I feel we had a very productive session, and I believe we are making good progress.

or

... you will understand why I cannot reveal what transpired in my conversations with them. However, I think everyone is demonstrating a willingness to be reasonable and to cooperate in bringing the matter forward.

Conversely, if the mediator is given permission to reveal certain matters, it is vital that he or she should expressly state this when revealing the information: 'Don Panic has permitted me to reveal to you that ...' The reasons for this are similar to those above: by expressing the permission to disclose certain matters, the mediator can prevent Major Stress being misled into believing that an indiscretion or breach of confidence has just taken place.

The fact that confidentiality is a cornerstone of the mediation process may frequently produce its own problems. Take the following situations:

- Major Stress reveals to the mediator, in confidence, that the current state of the floor is such as could possibly lead to the collapse of the building at that level – but asks the mediator not to pass that on to Don Panic
- the mediator, when in caucus with Major Stress, accidentally lets slip the details of the Book Fair to Major Stress, after having been specifically instructed by Don Panic to keep it secret at that stage
- the mediator has misunderstood an important element of the case put forward by Major Stress and, as a result, has misrepresented the issues to Don Panic in one of the caucus sessions; this has lead to Don Panic and his team walking out of the mediation
- after the mediation process has been going for several hours

and the parties are close to settlement, the mediator suddenly remembers where he has seen Major Stress before – in court 20 years ago, when he was suing Major Stress for a defective floor

The first principle in answer to most ethical issues arising during a mediation is that the issue must be addressed. No ethical problem should be ignored, passed over, swept under the carpet or allowed to fester. Delay in dealing with the matter can simply serve to exacerbate it and render it more difficult for the mediator to confront it later or to extricate himself or herself from any problem it has caused.

INFORMATION DISCLOSING RISK OF HARM

In relation to the first of the above scenarios, the duty on the part of the mediator is relatively clear: where he or she acquires information which relates or gives rise to a material risk of harm, injury or other risk to safety, the mediator may – or indeed must – proceed on the basis that the duty of confidentiality has been terminated and no longer applies. In most cases, the mediator will have ensured that a clause to this effect was inserted in the Mediation Agreement.

However, although the confidentiality of the process may have been suspended or terminated by the disclosure of some risk of harm, the mediator must nevertheless proceed carefully and sensitively. He or she should first secure some agreement from the party or parties as to the manner and extent of any disclosure to be made. The mediator will thus need to say something along the following lines:

You must understand that I simply cannot keep this information confidential. May I refer you to Clause 00 of the Mediation Agreement. If there is a material risk of harm, then I am obliged to disclose it and, in this case, I feel obliged to warn Don Panic accordingly. I will not divulge anything until you have had a brief opportunity to consider precisely how you would wish that information to be made known or how the warning is to be given. We will all then need to consider how this affects our mediation today and whether we feel able to continue.

ACCIDENTAL BREACH OF CONFIDENCE BY THE MEDIATOR

There will be many occasions during a mediation when the mediator will wish that he or she had not said something, or that it should have been put in a different way, or that something further should have been added. The beauty of the informality of the mediation process is that, in most instances, such errors or slips can be readily rectified.

> I'm sorry, perhaps I should not have put it in such terms. Let me re-phrase that . . .
>
> That was not what I had intended to say. Let me put it to you again . . .
>
> Sorry, let's wind back the tape and start again . . .

In other instances, a slip of the tongue may be more serious and will not be capable of swift remedy by re-phrasing or 're-framing'. As stated above, if a confidence has been inadvertently breached, the issue must not be overlooked, in the hope that 'perhaps no one will notice' or 'perhaps it will not make any difference'. As soon as the mediator realizes that he or she has disclosed an item of information that was received in confidence, that fact must be raised and dealt with – with both parties.

> I am sorry, Major Stress, I did not have permission to disclose the existence of the Book Fair to you, and I have done so accidentally. I will need to inform Don Panic about this error on my part, and he may wish to consider how to proceed in the light of this development . . .

There are certain important effects and benefits of being open and honest about the breach of confidence, and in dealing with the issue immediately it arises:

• it emphasizes to both parties that the mediator takes the matter of confidentiality very seriously

- it can enhance the parties' trust in the mediator by indicating to them that any past or future breaches of confidence have not gone by – and will not go by – unacknowledged or undisclosed
- it can increase the confidence of the parties to be more frank and open, in the knowledge that the mediator is unlikely to make another blunder
- it may provide an opportunity for the mediator to move the matter forward in a different way:

> Well, now that Major Stress knows about the Book Fair, perhaps he may be more receptive to or more understanding of your needs and interests in this matter. Perhaps I can persuade him to look at it from your point of view...

> Major Stress will now see that with the Book Fair approaching and without you having a proper floor upon which to provide the venue, you both have an added common interest to see this dispute resolved.

MISREPRESENTATION BY THE MEDIATOR

The situation where the mediator has, whether through misunderstanding or otherwise, misrepresented one party's position so as to produce extreme consequences, is very similar – the error or misunderstanding must be addressed and rectified immediately. Even where it does not produce immediate drastic consequences, any attempt to gloss over it can rebound upon the mediator at a later stage: 'But I thought you said earlier that...'

By admitting that the fault is that of the mediator and not of the parties, the mediator may even create an additional 'bond' between the parties, by bringing them to the realization that even the mediator is fallible, and that they have *both* suffered as a result of the misunderstanding on the part of the mediator.

DISCLOSURE OF CONFLICT OF INTEREST

In addition to confidentiality, another cornerstone of the mediation process is *neutrality and independence*. It will always be imperative to disclose any actual or potential conflict of interest – at all stages of the mediation. In the early stages, or prior to the commencement of the mediation, any disclosure of an actual or potential conflict gives the parties an opportunity to consider whether it has any bearing or significance upon the conduct of the mediation. In most cases, the parties will simply express gratitude for the frank disclosure and confirm that they have no objection to the mediator continuing to act. In some cases, the mediator will need to persuade the parties that, notwithstanding the connection or conflict, he or she feels sure that the process can still be conducted with full impartiality and independence. In a small minority of cases, the parties may feel too adversely affected to be able to continue. This, however, may stem from a misunderstanding of the role of the mediator, confusing it with that of an arbitrator or judge.

If, as suggested in the above scenario, the mediator discovers a past connection with one of the parties at a late stage in the proceedings, or even just as they are about to sign the settlement agreement, he or she must disclose the information immediately. There will inevitably be a temptation on the part of the mediator to 'just keep quiet about it', especially if it follows a long day of many hours of hard negotiation and mediation.

However, the dangers of saying nothing in the hope that the information will not emerge or materialize are too great. If Major Stress were to discover the connection subsequently, after having signed the agreement; if he were in the slightest way dissatisfied or if in some way he had become disenchanted with the settlement, it would enable him to seek a complete unravelling or nullifying of the agreement reached.

Most of the above situations can be catered for in the Mediation Agreement, so that when the situation arises, the mediator can rely upon and refer the parties back to the relevant parts of the agreement.

LIABILITY OF THE MEDIATOR

It is also usual for the Mediation Agreement to contain 'Disclaimer or Exclusion Clauses', whereby the mediator can seek to protect him or herself from claims in negligence or breach of contract. The mediator can also attempt to prevent the parties from calling him or her as a witness in any future litigation, by inserting a suitable clause to that effect. The validity or effectiveness of such exclusion clauses has not been fully tested in the English courts and the debate continues as to what should be the Court's approach in such circumstances.

Bibliography

[*Some legal publications are referred to using conventional legal citations*]

Adler, A. (1938) *Social Interest: A Challenge to Mankind*. London: Faber & Faber.

Alfini, J. J. (1991) 'Trashing, Bashing, Hashing: Is This the End of Good Mediation?' *19 Florida State University Law Review* 47.

Alfini, J. J., Press, S. B., Sternlight, J. R. and Stulberg, J. B. (2001) *Mediation Theory and Practice*. New York: Lexis.

Ansbacher, L. and Ansbacher, R. (1964) *The Individual Psychology of Alfred Adler*. New York, Hagerstown, San Francisco and London: Harper Torchbook (Harper & Row).

Armstrong, A. H. (1949) *An Introduction to Ancient Philosophy*. London: Methuen.

Aureli, F. and de Waal, F. B. M. (2000) 'Why Natural Conflict Resolution', in Aureli, F. and de Waal, F. B. M. (eds) *Natural Conflict Resolution*: Berkeley: University of California Press

Birke, R. and Fox, C. (1999) 'Psychological Principles in Negotiating Civil Settlements', *4 Harvard Negotiations Law Review* 1.

Boulle, L. and Nesic, M. (2001) *Mediation Principles, Process, Practice*. London: Butterworth.

Brunet, E. and Craver, C. B. (1997) *Alternative Dispute Resolution: The Advocate's Perspective*. Charlottesville, VA: Michie (Lexis).

Cohn, H. (1997) *Existential Thoughts and Therapeutic Practice*. London: Sage.

185

Condlin, R. J. (1992) 'Bargaining in the Dark', *51 Maryland Law Review* 1.

Cooper, M. (2003) *Existential Therapies*. London: Sage.

Cords, M. and Aureli, F. (2000) 'Reconciliation and Relationship Qualities', in Aureli, F. and de Waal, F. B. M. (eds) *Natural Conflict Resolution*. Berkeley: University of California Press.

Coser, L. A. (1956) *The Function of Social Conflict*. New York: Free Press.

Craver, C. B. (2001) *Effective Legal Negotiation and Settlement*, 4th edn. New York: Lexis.

Darwin, C. (1859) *The Origin of Species*. London: Murray.

de Bono, Edward (1995) *Conflicts*. Harmondsworth: Penguin.

Descartes, R. (1968) *Discourse on Method and The Meditations*. London: Penguin.

Deutsch, M. (1973) *The Resolution of Conflict*. New Haven and London: Yale University Press.

Durant, W. (1962) *Outline of Philosophy, Plato to Russell*. London: Ernest Benn Ltd.

Fisher, R. and Ury, W. (1981) *Getting to Yes: Negotiating Agreement Without Giving In*. Boston: Houghton Mifflin.

Freud, S. (1979) *On Psychopathology*. Harmondsworth: Penguin.

Goodpaster, G. (1996) 'A Primer on Competitive Bargaining', *Journal of Dispute Resolution* 325.

Heaton, J. M. (2002) 'The Human Body Is the Best Picture of the Human Soul', *13.2 Journal of the Society for Existential Analysis*.

Izard, C. (1991) *The Psychology of Emotions*. New York and London: Plenum Press.

Kirkegaard, S. (1968) *Concluding Unscientific Postscript*. Princeton, NJ: Princeton University Press.

Korda, M. (1975) *Power: How to Get It, How to Use It*. New York: Random House.

Law Commission (1994) 'Personal Injury Compensation: How Much Is Enough?' *Law Commission Report*, No. 225.

Lazarus, R. S. (1991) *Emotion and Adaptation*. New York: Oxford University Press.

Lewis, J. (1997) 'Unnecessary Caution', *97 Law Society Gazette* 123.

Love, L. (1997) 'Top Ten Reasons Why a Mediator Should Not Evaluate', *24 Florida State University Law Review* 937.

Lundin, R. (1989) *Alfred Adler's Basic Concepts and Implications*. Muncie, IN: Accelerated Development Inc.

Mackie, K. and Marsh, W. (1995) *Commercial Dispute Resolution*. London: Butterworth.

Mnookin, R. (1993) 'Why Negotiations Fail: An Exploration of Barriers to the Resolution of Conflict', *8 Ohio State Journal* 235.

Mnookin, R. and Ross, L. (1995) *Barriers to Conflict Resolution*, 2, K. Arrow, R. Mnookin, L. Ross and R. Wilson. (eds). New York: Norton.

Palmer, M. and Roberts, S. (1988) *Dispute Processes*. London: Butterworth.

Perls, F. (1969) *Gestalt Theory Verbatim*. New York and London: Bantam Books

Randolph, P. (2000) 'Scepticism about Mediation', *150 New Law Journal* 565.

Riskin L. (1984) 'Toward Newer Standards for the Neutral Mediator', *26 Arizona Law Review* 329.

Riskin, L. (1994) 'Mediator Orientations, Strategies and Techniques, Alternatives', *1 Harvard Negotiation Law Review* 7 (23–4).

Rogers, C. (1987) 'Speaking Personally', in *The Carl Rogers Reader*. London: Constable.

Sacks, Jonathan (2002) *The Dignity of Difference*. London: Continuum.

Salamon, R. (1993) *Handbook of Emotions*. New York and London: Guildford Press.

Sartre, J. P. (1958) *Being and Nothingness*. London: Routledge.

Scott, B. (1981) *The Skills of Negotiating*. London: Wildwood House.

Simmel, G. (1955) *Conflict*, trans. Kurt H. Wolff. Glencoe, IL: Free Press.

Slaikeu, K. (1996) *When Push Comes to Shove: A Practical Guide to Mediating Disputes*. Indianapolis: Jossey-Bass.

Slavin, M. and Kriegman, D. (1992) *The Adaptive Design of the Human Psyche*. New York and London: Guildford Press.

Spinelli, E. (1989) *The Interpreted World*. London: Sage.

Stillinger, C. *et al.* (1988) 'The Reactive Devaluation Barrier to Conflict Resolution', Working Paper No. 3, Series 1. Stanford, CA: Stanford Center on Conflict Negotiation.

Strasser, F. (1999) *Emotions*. London: Duckworth.

Strasser, F. and Strasser, A. (1997) *Existential Time-limited Therapy*. Chichester: Wiley.

Stulberg, J. B. (1981) 'The Theory and Practice of Mediation: An Answer to Susskind', *6 Vermont Law Review* 85.

Susskind, L. (1981) 'Environmental Mediation and the Accountability Problem', *6 Vermont Law Review* 1.

Tversky, A. and Kahneman, D. (1991) ' Loss Aversion in Riskless Choice', **106** *Quarterly Journal of Economics* 1039.

van de Riet, V., Korb, P. and Gorrell, J. J. (1980) *Gestalt Theory: An Introduction*. Oxford: Pergamon Press.

van Deurzen, E. (1987) 'Existential Therapy' in *Individual Therapy in Britain* edited by Windy Dryden. Harper & Row: London.

van Schaik C. P. (2000) 'The Natural History of Valuable Relationships in Primates' in Aureli, F. and de Waal, F. B. M. *Natural Conflict Resolution*. Berkeley: University of California Press.

Walton, C. (2001) *Charlesworth and Percy on Negligence*, (2001), 10th edn. London: Sweet & Maxwell.

Weckstein, D. T. (1997) 'In Praise of Party Empowerment', **33** *Williamette Law Review* 501.

Index